LITTLE MISS

Nate

LITTLE MISS

a father, his daughter & rocket science

NATHAN MEIKLE

ABOUT THE COVER

One day, while Kyla and I were reading a favorite book, we took a picture. The next day, while reading a different favorite book, we took another picture. Those pictures, along with hundreds of others, eventually became the cover of *Little Miss*.

PRAISE FOR NATHAN MEIKLE'S
LITTLE MISS

"*Little Miss* is a wonderful book that could change your life—and the lives of your children and grandchildren. It is the touching, provocative story of a father struggling to give his daughter one of life's greatest gifts: a love of learning. And yet *Little Miss* is so much more. It's a story about sacrifice, achievement, guilt, happiness, grief and love—in other words, it's a story about life. First-time father and author, Nathan Meikle, is poised to inspire countless parents to read more to their children, and in the process, alter the destinies of families for generations to come. After reading this book, I want to help this cause. Children who love learning become parents who love learning, and parents who love learning pass that on to their children. *Little Miss* has implications for policy makers, educators, community members, parents, grandparents and anyone else with an interest in children. In sum, this book is for all of us. I wish *Little Miss* had been written 27 years ago when I first became a parent. But even though I couldn't benefit from it then, I hope my children will benefit from it now—I'm giving each of them a copy. And I'm betting you will want to share *Little Miss* with others as well."

—**Stephen M. R. Covey**, father of five
and author of *The Speed of Trust*

CONTENTS

It's 7:00 a.m. and I'm asleep. Crack! The bedroom door flies open, slamming the wall. As I try to gain consciousness, I hear footsteps running toward the bed. My eyes fire open just in time to see Kyla jump on the bed next to me.

"Dad, can we get a Bill Nye about private parts? I want to know why I have nipples."

LITTLE MISS

Once you learn to read, you will be forever free.
—Frederick Douglass

Day 150

Introduction

M y daughter Kyla sits in her high chair at the dinner table—straps around her legs, tray on her lap. She doesn't realize she's a captive. All of her attention is on the kindergarten reading program she's about to finish.

"Now…we…can…play…says…tic…toc." She reads each word slowly while bobbing her head in rhythm.

"Last page!" I say. Kyla kicks her feet back and forth in excitement. Our experiment is working. At least in the short run.

Kyla is two years old.

"To…g…e…t," she says slowly, sounding out each letter, "…get…a…pl…pl…p…" She is struggling with the word *pal,* and suddenly points to it and says confidently, "That's one you just have to memorize." My wife, Keshia, laughs, and I smile at Kyla's comment—it's the same phrase we repeat to Kyla each time she comes across a new sight word. I quickly correct her though, "No, this word you can actually sound out."

Kyla continues, this time without hesitation, "p..a..l. Pal!"

"To get a pal," I repeat.

"You…need…to…be…a…pal."

"KYLAAAAAAAAAAA! I shout, as Kyla covers her mouth in excitement. "DOUBLE FIVE! YOU DID THE WHOLE PROGRAM!"

Kyla raises her hands and hits mine. I hug and kiss her while Keshia shouts, "KYLA, KYLA, KYLAAAAA!"

"And now where are we going?" I ask. "Where do you get to go now?"

Kyla thinks for a moment and then shouts, "CIRCUS!" while jolting her body and hands upward toward me.

"CIRCUS!" I repeat in excitement.

I unstrap her, and she walks to the progress chart hanging on the wall. She moves the marker to the "I DID IT" spot. I never expected the progress chart to be so powerful.

When we started this experiment five months earlier, Keshia and I had no indication that Kyla was anything but average. Even now, our opinion remains unchanged—we're convinced that other children will achieve similar results by using the same techniques. Whether the benefits of the techniques outweigh the costs is the more difficult question.

I hug Kyla one more time and say, "Now what do we get to do?"

She thinks for a moment. "Read the new ones!"

The first-grade reading program is on the couch.

*To see a video clip of this scene, scan the following QR code:

There are many little ways to enlarge your child's world. Love of books is the best of all. —Jacqueline Kennedy

Day 0

Earlier Is Better, Except When It Isn't

"So you don't really want to teach Kyla this reading program," I say to Keshia. My less-than-subtle jab connects.

"I didn't say that," Keshia corrects me. "I said, 'I'll try to do it.'" Keshia's feeling the tension but doing her best to act like she isn't. Anything to avoid confrontation. Her temperament is rarely inconsistent with her petiteness.

"Yeah, but we both know there's a big difference between trying and doing," I respond. "I've been trying to lose ten pounds for a year," I say with a faint smile, hoping Keshia recognizes my small concession. I don't mean for this discussion to become heated; I'm a little surprised at my own ambition. Up until an hour ago, when my sister gifted us the reading program, I had never even considered teaching Kyla to read. Now I'm getting upset at Keshia for being too passive?

I continue, "I just don't understand your hesitation. What's the downside?"

"And I don't understand your zealousness. Kyla's two! She won't even start kindergarten for three more years." Well, not anything to avoid confrontation.

"Look, I know she's young—maybe too young. But if this program works, if we can teach her to read at age two, why wait? The earlier the better."

"You don't know that earlier is better, Nate."

"Earlier helped all of those hockey players in *Outliers*," I respond.

Maybe "accumulative advantage," the effect described in Malcolm Gladwell's *Outliers* is driving my newfound ambition. Seventy percent of elite Canadian hockey players have birthdays in the first half of the year. As children, the players with birthdays between January and June were bigger and stronger than those with birthdays later in the year. And because the older children were bigger and stronger, they were selected to more travel teams and played more hockey, creating a virtuous cycle. A small advantage early in life can lead to a large advantage later—an accumulative advantage.

"Yeah, but Nate," Keshia responds, "I don't care if our kids are average."

Touché. Several weeks ago we listened to comedian Steve Carell talk about his children: "Everyone else's kids are the cutest, smartest, nicest, fastest, or biggest. My kids are just average. I still love 'em, but there's not a single thing special about them." We'd never admired Steve Carell more.

"Look, I'll love Kyla whether she's the first one picked or the last. But I don't think this is about my ego."

"Well what's the downside in waiting—letting her learn to read when *she's* ready? You didn't learn to read when you were two, and you turned out fine."

"Yeah, but you know I hate that argument. I don't want her to turn out 'fine,' and I don't want to be just a 'fine' dad. I want her to be the best *she* can be. Just because I'm 'fine' doesn't mean I couldn't be better."

"Yeah, but it doesn't mean you couldn't be worse."

Oddly enough, I had always done worse in school than Keshia, and now I was the one pushing education. Keshia was the high school valedictorian—the one who stayed up late doing AP calculus. I was the ignorant jock—writing my state-required senior essay on "Why fat chicks shouldn't wear tight clothes." But maybe that's why

I was suddenly so intent on pushing education. I didn't want Kyla to be like me. Certainly not the high school me.

"Look, Keshia, I'm talking about doing the program—lovingly—for just a few minutes per day. Persistently, but not forcefully."

"Like I said earlier, I'll try the program. But I'm not looking for more things to do with Kyla."

"Well, what if I head it up?" I say. "You can just supervise me—make sure I don't turn into the 'overambitious parent.'"

Keshia nods her head. "That's fine with me."

"Okay," I say, wondering how to fit the program into my schedule. "I'll start tomorrow."

Wear the old coat and buy the new book.
—Austin Phelps

Day 0 Bedtime

Ignorance Was Bliss

*W*hen do children learn to read? Age Three? Five? Seven? I'm lying in bed at my parents' home in Idaho Falls. Spring break has just begun, the 15-hour drive from our home in San Francisco behind us.

Should Kyla know the alphabet by now? Should she recognize simple words? Is she already behind? I climb out of bed, and pull out my computer.

A quick Google search puts my mind at ease. Most children don't learn to read until kindergarten, typically at age five or six. Relieved that Kyla is not behind I still feel a twinge of guilt—I've been

Kyla's dad for two years and never considered if I should teach her to read, let alone how.

I shift my Google search to "how to teach children to read" and come across *The Read-Aloud Handbook* by Jim Trelease. The book isn't a "How to teach your child to read" but rather a "How to teach your child to *want* to read." And the reviews on Amazon are gushing—a 22-year-veteran elementary-school teacher calling the Trelease book the "finest book about what reading could and should be."

I jump to the negative reviews. Trelease is overreaching, according to the first review, relying on anecdotal evidence and logically unsound arguments. Yet the book is still worth the money, claims the reviewer, because of the book recommendations in the index.

I read several more reviews and place my order. Worst case I'll benefit from the book recommendations in the index—in the so-called "Treasury of Read-Alouds."

I shut off the computer and climb back into bed, oblivious to how much Trelease is about to transform our lives.

April 1999 - Ten years before Kyla's birth

"Nate, we want you to play football for us," Coach Haun said as he slid the scholarship offer across the table. I had done it. My first, and only, scholarship offer. For just a moment I forgot that it was a partial scholarship to a junior college in rural Idaho. But given that I was coming from public-high-school-small-town Idaho, the scholarship was fitting.

Just as quickly as the excitement came, it left. Coach Haun was making a mistake. Every other college football coach in the country knows I'm not good enough to play college football.

"If God knows what number I'm going to think of next, how am I free to choose my own number?" My eight-year old brain cannot reconcile the difference between a God who knows the future and a God who doesn't predestine it.

"Think about your dog Sandy," my father replies. "You know she loves to play fetch. In fact, you know her so well that you know what will happen if you throw a ball—she will fetch it. Sandy is still free to choose—you just know what she will choose."

But if I'm the one throwing the ball, is Sandy still free?

Day 1

My Baby Can What?

"Kyla, do you want to watch a movie?" I've thrown a ball and know exactly what Kyla will do next.

"Yes! Yes! Yes! Yes! Yes!" she chants as she sprints into the living room, plopping herself in front of the television, unaware of the sudden rule change allowing her to watch movies sometime other than during long car rides.

I agreed with Keshia to not force the reading program on Kyla. But in this moment, is Kyla still free?

"Kyla, we're going to watch an educational movie today. It's going to teach you how to read." Kyla glances at me and then flashes her eyes back to the television, nodding all the while. And panting. I'm certain the only word she heard was "movie." Keshia is looking on, intrigued.

"In fact, Kyla, we get to watch this movie every day now" I say. The program, *Your Baby Can Read (YBCR)*, recommends showing the 20-minute video twice per day which seems extreme. Though I am technically not disregarding the American Academy of Pediatrics' recommendation of no screen time for children under two—Kyla is two and a half—I feel guilty encouraging Kyla to up her screen time.

The movie begins. "Hi" appears on the screen in big letters. A black arrow runs underneath the word, moving left to right at the same time a child's voice says, "Hi."

"Clap" appears next, the black arrow running underneath the word as a child says the word. A child is then shown clapping her hands for five seconds.

"Nose" followed by the arrow, the voice, the video.

"This is the program?" I think to myself. Where's the animation? The silly voices? The catchy songs? Are we really watching flashcards on TV?

"Ooh Kyla, look at the word *arms*," I say feigning excitement.

Kyla isn't fooled. She's now looking around the room for something else to do.

"Ooh Kyla, *arms up*."

Kyla looks at the screen momentarily and then jumps to her feet and runs to the closet where she had been playing with a puzzle.

I look at Keshia, and she shrugs.

So we won't be teaching Kyla to read quite yet. But one thing is clear—Kyla is still free.

No matter how busy you may think you are, you must find time for reading, or surrender yourself to self-chosen ignorance. —Confucius

Day 2

Watch and Learn

"Kyla, check this out!" I am holding a set of 16 flashcards that came with the *Your Baby Can Read* program. If the video can't keep her attention, maybe I can.

"Look Kyla, *nose*," I say, running my finger along the bottom of the card that says *nose* in big black letters. I flip the card over and show Kyla a picture of a boy touching his nose. "I'm going to steal your nose" I say in my zombie voice as I reach for her nose. Kyla pulls back and giggles, "Noooo, don't take my nose" she laughs, as she covers her nose with her hands.

I flip to the next card. "Look Kyla, *clap*," I say, while running my finger under the word. I then flip the card over to a picture of a boy clapping. "I'm going to clap your feet, Kyla!" I growl. This time Kyla sticks her feet out for me to clap while she giggles.

According to the instructions, the reading program requires virtually no effort from Kyla—she just needs to watch me perform.

And watch me she does. Sixteen words later, we finish the first set. The program itself isn't innovative, but the idea behind it is. Kyla can learn to read, or at least memorize words, by watching me. I just need to figure out how to make her want to.

September 1999 - Ten years before Kyla's birth

Why do my friends think they are going to be stars? Football practices had just begun and I knew I would be sipping Gatorade from the bench all season. Yet, I believed that I was more talented than some of my most confident friends. Who's right?

My questions became moot when my knee bent sideways in practice. Season over. Next up—a two-year hiatus to South America as a missionary.

Children are made readers on the laps of their parents. —Emilie Buchwald

Sometimes, you read a book and it fills you with this weird evangelical zeal, and you become convinced that the shattered world will never be put back together unless and until all living humans read the book. —John Green

Day 3

Trelease Treasury

The Trelease book arrives and I start reading:

> You may have tangible wealth untold.
> Caskets of jewels and coffers of gold.
> Richer than I you can never be,
> I had a mother who read to me.
> — Strickland Gillian

I know I should read to Kyla. I also know I should exercise daily.

I used to love reading to Kyla from her favorite book, *My Nursery Rhymes Collection*—but her threshold for repetitiveness is 100x higher than mine. Though I haven't read to Kyla as much as I wish, I'm reminded of the Chinese proverb: "The best time to plant a tree is 20 years ago. The next best time is today."

I want Kyla to be a reader and, according to the extensive research Trelease cites, the single most important thing I can do is read to her.[1] Every read-aloud session teaches Kyla to read because children mimic parents. And if I can make reading enjoyable for her—and me—Kyla will associate pleasure with books. "What we teach children to love and desire will always outweigh what we teach them to do," goes the old adage.

And who wouldn't want their child to be a reader? "The last twenty-five years of reading research," writes Trelease, "confirms that…students who read the most, read the best, achieve the most, and stay in school the longest."

Learning to read is critical, but even more important is the ability to read to learn. If not for Dale Carnegie, I would still be self-conscious when talking to others. *Tuesdays with Morrie* taught me to embrace old age. Tolkien fed my imagination.

Hugo taught me compassion, and Tolstoy empathy. And Trelease is teaching me about reading.

I have always imagined that paradise will be a kind of library. —Jorge Luis Borges

Day 4

Darn It, Dad!

We drive to the Idaho Falls library to put the Trelease "Treasury" list to the test. I walk to the computer and start looking up books. Every time I find a book from the Treasury I'm surprised at the jolt of treasure-hunt serotonin I get. The jolts of anti-serotonin, however, are five times more frequent—most of the Treasury books are checked out.

I quit looking for Treasury books and start browsing. This leads to even more frustration because I am overwhelmed with options.

I quit looking for books altogether, check out the few Treasury books I did find, and head back to my parent's home.

Once home I ask Kyla if she wants to read some of the library books we picked out.

"Can we read this one first?" she asks, handing me a random book from the bag.

"Sure. This book is called *The Fleas Sneeze*." I open the book and begin reading about a group of animals in a barn. All of the animals are asleep, except the flea that is wide-awake with a cold.

"Does eddybody hab a tissue for be?" I read, as I pretend to sniffle. Kyla giggles, as she helps me turn the page…

And the next page…

And next one.

The flea eventually sneezes, waking up all of the animals in the barn. I jolt Kyla, and she gives me a quick laugh and is already helping me turn the page. All of the animals soon fall back asleep when the hog sniffles, "I think I'b godda sdeeze."

"Again!" Kyla shouts.

"How bout we do….this alligator book instead," I say, pulling *Snip Snap! What's That?* from the bag. Kyla nods, her eyes focused on the alligator.

"When the alligator came *creeping*," I whisper, "*…creeping…creeping* up the stairs, were the children scared?" I turn the page.

"YOU BET THEY WERE!" I shout. Kyla jumps a little, but still keeps her eyes on the book.

Trelease is two for two.

We read several more books, all of them entertaining, and the read-aloud session ends.

"We can read later tonight," I say, "but now I need to get back to studying." I am in my second year of law school and need to make up for the morning playdate.

"Oh darn it, Dad."

June 2000 - Nine years before Kyla's birth

So much for my scholarship. One month into my mission my friend notified me that our junior college was dropping all athletic programs. Is it even possible to lateral from rural Idaho? I would have gladly dropped down a level had it been possible to go lower.

No entertainment is so cheap as reading, nor any pleasure so lasting. —Lady Montagu

Day 8

Letter Factory

"**K**yla, guess what I have for you," I say excitedly from the living room.

"It's not Kyla!" she responds, as she walks up the stairs. "It's Minnie Lillie Rapunzel Aurora Tinker Bell Simba!"

"Sorry about that Lillie Minnie Jasmine Cinderella Simba Bell Tinker," I respond. "I have a new movie for you to watch."

I recently purchased, *LeapFrog: Letter Factory,* a clever cartoon that teaches the alphabet. Whereas *YBCR* teaches memorization, *Letter Factory* teaches phonics. The two videos seem like perfect complements.

"Can I watch it right now?" Kyla responds.

"Not quite. But we can watch it in the car today." We are about to start the trek from Idaho back to California.

"But there's only one condition," I continue. "Before we watch the new video, we have to watch the 'flash card' video." Though Kyla loves doing the manual flashcards with Elmo, Cookie Monster, and Ariel—all played by me—she is yet to make it through an entire *YBCR* flash card video.

"But I want to watch the new video first," Kyla says with a whimper.

"Belle, we're going to be in the car all day today. You can watch the new video *Letter Factory* today, but you have to watch the 'flash card' video first." I'm not forcing Kyla to watch the flash card video—she simply has to decide how bad she wants to watch *Letter Factory.*

On second thought, this probably is coercion.

When we get into the car, Kyla relents and we turn on the flash card video. Kyla sits in the back seat, eyes glued to the screen—in complete silence. For twenty minutes.

The instant the flashcard video ends Kyla says, "Can I watch the new video now?" She did it— watched the entire flashcard video.

I put in *Letter Factory* and Kyla is laughing within minutes. The main character, Professor Quigley, walks a talking frog to the "A" room. Quigley, dressed like a monster, bursts through the door yelling, "Oooga Booga Wooga." The A's inside the room all shout "Aah!" to which Quigley responds, "That's right. The "A" says 'aah.'" I now know what I will say when I walk into Kyla's room tomorrow morning.

Twenty-five letter rooms later, Kyla says the word I knew would be coming: "Again!"

As predictable as my dog Sandy.

"You can watch the video again, but next we have to listen to a few books on tape," I say as I pull out the iPod and scroll to Kyla's playlist. "How about *Diary of a Spider, Bink and Gollie*, and *Bark, George.*"

"Okay," Kyla mumbles.

The books on tape are followed by music, games, and a nap, and then the routine starts over again, repeating itself several times during the day.

*****

"Dad," Kyla says faintly from the back seat. We are pulling into San Francisco—the fifteen-hour drive behind us—and are met with a thunder storm. Kyla has been in the nap stage of the routine for several hours. I don't immediately respond, hoping Kyla will go back to sleep for the remaining few minutes of the drive.

"Dad," Kyla says again softly. "Can you turn the lightnings off?"

You're the same today as you'll be in five years except for the people you meet and the books that you read. —Charlie "Tremendous" Jones

Day 10

Reservationless

Given our library failure last time, I try a new approach to checking out books. While sitting in a chair at home, I log on to the Palo Alto library catalogue and search for Mo Willems, an apparently popular author my friend recommended to me.

The library carries 57 unique titles by Willems, 255 total copies, but only 17 are checked in—across five different branches. I'm more likely to die in a car accident on the way to the library than find a popular Mo Willems book at the library.

I start reserving copies. Pure serotonin. I then reserve a dozen Trelease "Treasury" books. More serotonin. I also Google "Best Children Books" and reserve a dozen of those.

Rather than go to the library and look for books that aren't in, the library can contact me when the books are available.

September 2001 - Eight years before Kyla's birth

I was wrong—my friends were right. While walking the streets of Iquique, Chile, I was reading a newspaper article that my father had mailed me. Several of my former teammates had earned athletic scholarships to Division I programs. If they can do it...

If you're in a card game and don't know who the sucker is, stand up and leave. It's you. —Poker Aphorism

Day 17

Twenty-five Birds in the Hand

At the library we pick up our stack of 25 free books that are patiently waiting for us. Once I have the 25 books in my bag, browsing for more books is simply icing. I no longer stress about picking out boring books because I already have 25 winners in the bag. I then realize that on my first trip to the library several weeks ago, I was the sucker. The books that are checked in are, by definition, the ones nobody wants.

Oh, magic hour, when a child first knows she can read printed words! — Betty Smith

Day 18

Sooner Is Not Better, Except When It Is

"Kyla, you can read!" I shout. Kyla has read "clap" correctly two different times now. Keshia claps and Kyla grins and shrugs her shoulders.

Kyla especially enjoys flashcards now that her brain makes sense of them. Trelease on the other hand is less pleased with our methods: "For the parent who thinks sooner is better, who has an eighteen-month-old child barking at flash-cards, my response is: *Sooner is not better*. Are the dinner guests who arrive an hour early better guests than those who arrive on time? Of course not."[2]

NATHAN MEIKLE

Trelease's use of the word "barking" seemingly sums up his position on flash cards. I can understand why he is against forcing children to do flashcards, but what if Kyla enjoys it? I also don't buy the "dinner guests" analogy. Sometimes dinner guests who arrive early—and help set up for example—are better than dinner guests who arrive on time. What if learning to read early *is* better for some children?

Louis Auchincloss, in the *Rector of Justin,* describes an educator who is criticized for his teaching methods. The educator responds that the "only thing a teacher has to go on is that rare spark in a boy's eye. And when you see that...you're an [expletive] if you worry where it comes from. Whether it's an ode of Horace or an Icelandic saga or something that goes boom in a laboratory."

I see the spark in Kyla's eye now that she has just read her first word. Should I care if it is a flashcard that gives it to her?

But what if Trelease is right? Kyla seems to enjoy the flashcards, but maybe she's just doing it to please me. Maybe I am pressuring her more than I realize. Maybe this is all too much too soon and will backfire down the road. Trelease has gained enough credibility with me that I at least want to research what experts say about teaching toddlers to read.

Regardless of Trelease's stance on early literacy, he has inspired me to read to Kyla more—10x more—and I have no reservations about this. The more we read, the broader her vocabulary becomes. And according to research, the prime predictor of success for children entering kindergarten is a broad vocabulary.

Trelease cites a well-known study[3] in which researchers studied 42 families from varying socioeconomic statuses. All parents said and did basically the same things for their children, with one glaring exception: those parents from the higher socioeconomic status talked to their children more—a whole lot more. The daily number of words for each family was then projected across four years and children from the highest socioeconomic status will have heard 48 million words compared to children from the lowest socioeconomic status, who will have heard only 13 million words. It's not hard to guess which child will understand the kindergarten teacher better.

Additionally, reading a book to a child exposes the child to three times as many rare words as a regular conversation does, and 50% more rare words than a television show. Reading to Kyla is its own reward, to say nothing of potential intellectual benefits.

We're now taking a three-pronged approach to teaching Kyla to read. First is memorization with *YBCR*. Second is phonics with the *Leap Frog* DVD's. And third is reading aloud to Kyla—a lot.

Above all, I just want to make reading fun for Kyla. But good books make that easy. After reading several *Elephant and Piggie* books, by Mo Willems, I'm the one who has to put an end to the read-aloud session. *Chickens to the Rescue, Pigs to the Rescue* and *Cows to the Rescue* by John Himmelman, get me clucking, squealing and mooing in ways Keshia knew she'd never hear from me. And *Little Pea*, *Little Oink*, and *Little Hoot*, all by Amy Krouse Rosenthal, turn Kyla's world upside down; what two-year old doesn't enjoy reading books about peas that don't like candy, pigs that aren't allowed to clean their rooms and owls that have to stay up late?

"If you don't like to read," said J.K. Rowling, "you haven't found the right book."

June 2002 - Seven years before Kyla's birth

*"We'd love for you to join our football team,"
Coach Kilts said. I was home from South America
visiting a junior college in rural Utah—enrollment
3000. A lateral transfer might be possible after all.
Kilts continued, "But we don't have a full
scholarship for you."*

Close enough.

"Now! Let's have a real good talk" reduces everyone to silence. —C.S. Lewis

Day 25

Book Baskets

"How would you feel about putting books on our dinner table?" I ask Keshia while we are sitting in the living room. Kyla is in bed and we are enjoying our sacred two hours of peace.

"Why the table? What's wrong with the bag they're in?"

"Nothing's wrong with where they're at. And I'm not saying I want to put all of the library books on the table, just a few. Trelease recommends putting book baskets on the table, in the bathroom, and next to Kyla's bed as a way to encourage reading." Trelease has already gained credibility in our home thanks to the "treasury" recommendations, but I am about to find out if his credibility has limits.

"Yeah, I don't know about the table," Keshia responds. "I'm okay with the book basket by the bed, although I wouldn't want the books to keep Kyla from napping. Regarding the bathroom..." Her voice trails off while she thinks.

"I'm actually against the bathroom basket," I interject. "Disposable magazines are great for the bathroom. Books less so."

"Yeah, I agree," Keshia says.

"When I first read about the table basket," I continue "I was skeptical. But the more I think about it, the more I think it would be fun to read during meals."

"Oh." Keshia responds with a hint of surprise. "So we're discussing two different points then— whether we should physically put books on the table to encourage reading and whether we should read during meal time?"

I realize that I have made a logical jump—books on the table is one thing, interrupting family dinner a whole other ball game.

"I think reading during meal times could be fun, especially given all the great books we are finding," I say.

"Yeah but what about Kyla's food?"

Kyla is already having a difficult time staying focused long enough to finish a meal. The last thing Keshia wants is another distraction.

"Yeah I've been thinking about that," I say, "and I wonder if reading during meal times could improve her eating habits. Rather than getting bored so quickly, she might be willing to stay at the table longer—actually finish her food."

"Another distraction is going to *improve* her eating habits?" Keshia responds.

"I don't know. I admit that it might make things worse. But there is a chance that it improves things."

"Yeah and there's a chance she'll be 6 feet tall. Putting aside her eating habits though," Keshia continues, "I'm not sure I want library books disrupting our meal times." On the day we married, Keshia and I committed to always have family dinner together, so long as it was possible. As sacred as post-Kyla's-bedtime is, dinnertime is even more so.

"I don't want the books to disrupt our meals either," I respond, "but I have been wanting to read more to Kyla, and I only have a few chances during the day. Plus, the whole point of eating dinner together is to help us interact with each other. What better way to interact than by reading a few books together?"

"You're sure buying what Trelease is selling," Keshia says.

"I think it's an experiment worth trying. We can always stop if we don't like it."

Reading good books ruins you for enjoying bad books. —Mary Ann Shaffer

Day 45

Party Rock Language Dancing

Kyla routinely requests 5-10 books at each meal—her high score is 20. I now read her more books in a month than I used to read in an entire year—all thanks to Trelease. Finding "bat baby" in *The Day the Babies Crawled Away* is always a race. Watching *Dirty Gert* eat dirt makes Kyla squeal in disgust. Hearing *How Do You Wokka-Wokka?* makes her dance.

And every Trelease recommendation is a hit. I shouldn't have been surprised at how much more fun it is to read a good book than a bad one, or the "same ol' ones" for that matter. Shockingly, Kyla would rather listen to *Henry and the Crazed*

Chicken Pirates than to Keshia and I talk about the weather.

We wonder whether we read to Kyla too much, but come back to one question, "If Kyla wants us to read ten books at dinner, should we stop her?" So far our answer is, "That's a stupid question." Especially because the read-alouds launch into "language dancing" conversations (Why _did_ Pigeon want to drive the bus? Why _did_ Sylvester turn into a rock? Why _did_ the babies crawl away?).

Language dancing (back and forth conversation) when compared to talking at someone, is six times more powerful in promoting language development.[4] Every conversation with Kyla develops her synaptic pathways. The more pathways, and more refined those pathways, the faster and easier her thought patterns. But the benefits aren't linear. According to Harvard Professor Clayton Christensen:

> A child who has heard 48 million words in the first three years won't just have 3.7 times as many well-lubricated connections in its brain as a child who has heard only 13 million words. The effect on brain cells is exponential. Each brain cell can be connected to hundreds of other cells by as many as ten thousand synapses. That means children who have been exposed to

LITTLE MISS

extra talk have an almost incalculable cognitive advantage.[5]

And as much as I care about synapses and pathways, I care even more about emotional bonds—ten books per day, multiplied by 300 days per year, multiplied by several years, equals a bond you don't get by watching Disney.

And speaking of bonds, we recently implemented a free-play technique that turns parents into Dale Carnegie. In their book *Switch*, Chip and Dan Heath describe parent-child interaction therapy (PCIT), which has achieved staggering results. In the first step, parents are taught how to play with their children: 1) devote 100% attention to children—no cell phones 2) let the children lead the play session 3) don't command, criticize, or teach the children 4) don't ask questions 5) describe the child's behavior 6) bend like a reed and 7) enjoy the children.

There is magic in the words, "Oh, wow, look how you've commandeered our bathroom and covered the floor with snakes, towels, little people, shoes, tutus, computers, cars, markers, marbles, water, puzzles, food and library books." That's a language dancing launching point—especially when my cell phone is in my pocket. And criticism kills conversations. So be it if Kyla wants to marry me three times per day while listening to Rapunzel sing "I See the Light." More power to her if she

41

thinks her magnets that she planted in a glass of water (that has been sitting on our kitchen table for the last three weeks) are going to grow into "magnet flowers." And if Kyla's listening to "Party Rock" downstairs and shouts, "Mom, come down and put your hands up to the sound!" Keshia now bends like a reed all the way to the living room.

December 2002 - Seven years before Kyla's birth

If I triple my output next year, I'll have a chance to play division I football. My first season in Utah—an average one—had just ended. No recruiters were calling.

The more that you read, the more things you will know. The more you learn, the more places you'll go. —Dr. Seuss

Day 55

Stupid Is Temporary

"Reading is an accrued skill," I read from the Trelease book. "Students who read the most, read the best."

And doing math homework helps you get good at math, I think to myself. I'm reminded of my first college math class when I came to a startling realization: I could do math. And I could do it well—so long as I did my homework and got help from tutors. I then had another startling realization: I shouldn't have dropped my high school math class after receiving a C; I should have just done my homework instead. I chose to quit when I could have chosen effort.

I continue reading Trelease: "The following formula can be documented. And though it doesn't hold true 100% of the time, it holds true far more often than not:

1. The more you read the more you know.
2. The more you know the smarter you grow.
3. The smarter you are, the longer you stay in school.
4. The longer you stay in school, the more diplomas you earn and the longer you are employed—thus the more money you earn in a lifetime.
5. The more diplomas you earn, the higher your children's grades will be in school.
6. The more diplomas you earn, the longer you live."[6]

This formula reminds me of a study on violinists. The best violinists relied on hard work, not innate talent, averaging 10,000 hours of deliberate practice over their lives compared to the next-best group which averaged just 7,500 hours, and the third best group which averaged only 5,000.

As important as "natural talent" might be, hours practiced can be even more important.

Kyla can memorize words rapidly, though her success seems to stem more from practice than genetics. People who practice memorizing words improve their ability to memorize words.

Ed Cooke, Grand Master of Memory, who can memorize a seventy-digit number in just over a minute, and a 1,000 digit number in less than an hour, claims that anyone else can do the same thing if they learn the techniques and work hard. When asked if he's a savant, Cooke responds that his memory is "quite average" and that a "photographic memory is a detestable myth."[7] When it comes to a world-class memory, effort and technique are more important than innate ability.

Research from Stanford professor Carol Dweck corroborates what Cooke believes:

> Society is obsessed with the idea of talent and genius and people who are 'naturals' with innate ability. People who believe in the power of talent tend not to fulfill their potential because they're so concerned with looking smart and not making mistakes. But people who believe that talent can be developed are the ones who really push, stretch, confront their own mistakes and learn from them.[8]

According to Dweck, individuals' mindsets can be placed on a continuum according to their views on where their talent originates. On one end of the spectrum are those who believe their abilities are fixed—the fixed mindset. On the other end are those people who believe in the importance of hard work—the growth mindset:

> In a fixed mindset students believe their basic abilities, their intelligence, their talents, are just fixed traits. They have a certain amount and that's that, and then their goal becomes to look smart all the time and never look dumb. In a growth mindset students understand that their talents and abilities can be developed through effort, good teaching and persistence. They don't necessarily think everyone's the same or anyone can be Einstein, but they believe everyone can get smarter if they work at it.[9]

"Kyla, you're smart," is a phrase we avoid. "Kyla, your hard work and persistence is paying off," is a phrase we look for excuses to use. I want to help Kyla develop a "growth mindset"—help her believe that her talent can be developed and that making mistakes is part of the process of growing. "If you're not making mistakes," said John Wooden, "then you're not doing anything."

"Why are you getting better at reading?" I often ask Kyla when we finish *YBCR*. She gets the answer right every time now: "Because I practice." It's for this reason—to encourage practice—that we turn on the subtitles every time Kyla watches a movie. Children in Finland are consistently among the world's best readers. Children in Finland also watch a lot of American television shows—with subtitles.

Had Keshia and I both had the growth mindset in high school we would have studied for the ACT rather than feared that a low score *after* studying would confirm what we were afraid of—that we were stupid.

It never occurred to us that our intelligence might not be fixed. Had only we believed Einstein: "It's not that I'm so smart, it's just that I stay with problems longer."

For unto every one that hath shall be given, and he shall have abundance: but from him that hath not shall be taken away even that which he hath.
—Matthew 25:29

Day 58

Reaping and Sowing

"Have you researched what the experts say about teaching toddlers to read?" Keshia asks me as I close my laptop and stand up to get ready for bed.

"Some, but I'm surprised at how little I've found," I respond as I sit back down on the couch next to Keshia. "Teaching toddlers to read has never really hit mainstream."

"So what have you found?"

"A lot of emotion and anecdote," I respond. "Not a lot of studies."

"So what are the criticisms?"

"Basically the same ones we've talked about: 'Don't push your kids or you'll burn them out' or 'Kids should be allowed to play, not forced to read.' Legitimate concerns, but given that Kyla enjoys the program and that we only do it for a few minutes per day…"

"Any other negatives?"

"*Your Baby Can Read* could theoretically make it more difficult for Kyla to learn phonics because she is memorizing whole words. But given that we're simultaneously teaching her phonics, I think this concern is mitigated. And even if she were disadvantaged, which I don't think she is, her "disadvantage" would be offset, at least partially, by the advantage she has already gained by reading whole words—especially because so few words in English can be sounded out phonetically."

"So are there any benefits of learning to read at age two?" Keshia asks.

"None documented, though I did come across a researcher from Toronto who recognized the Matthew Effect in reading ability."[10]

"Matthew Effect?" Keshia responds.

"Yeah, Chapter One in *Outliers,* the accumulative advantage effect—a small advantage early in life can lead to large advantages later in life."

"Oh yeah. The Canadian hockey players."

"Right," I respond. "This researcher from Toronto showed that the Matthew Effect is found in reading ability too. Early reading success typically leads to later reading success. And if children haven't learned to read by third grade, they could be in for a lifelong reading struggle."

"So you're still on board with all of this," Keshia responds, "even though there aren't any studies showing that it's beneficial?"

"I'm still on board with this because I don't think we should anchor our expectations to a government-sponsored education program that ranks mid to low in global standards. If we're going to make a mistake with Kyla, I'd rather err on the side of effort."

"Yeah, but not making a mistake is better than erring on a side," Keshia interjects.

"Right, but if Kyla practices reading," I continue, "and we can make it a good experience for her—she will get better at reading. And the better she gets, the more she will enjoy it, and the more she enjoys it, the more she will do it."

"Presumably," Keshia says.

"Right. Presumably. And the more she reads, the more she will learn."

"And the more she learns now, the more bored she will be in school later," says Keshia.

"True," I say, acknowledging that the issue isn't as cut and dry as I had just made it sound.

November 2003 - Six years before Kyla's birth

So much for a Division I scholarship. My other knee bent sideways during a game and now my sophomore season was over. Recruiters weren't calling, especially with my pending knee surgery.

There is no way to tell if a new children's classic has arrived until a generation or two has passed. The question isn't whether you'll read a book to your kids. It's whether they will read the same book to their kids, and so on down the line. —Eden Ross Lipson

Day 63

Monkey Brains

At the library I turn giddy when I see a childhood favorite, *Caps for Sale.* I snatch it off the shelf, thumb through the pages, and tell Keshia about the peddler who wore 17 caps on his head and the monkeys who took the caps and mocked the peddler saying, "Tss! Tss! Tss!"

After finishing the summary, I admit my embarrassment for having become so enthused about such a simple book. Keshia reminds me how excited she had become recently at seeing one of her childhood favorites—*The Little Mouse, the Red Ripe Strawberry, and the Big Hungry Bear*. Simple or not, childhood favorites do have the power to take us back in time.

At home I read *Caps for Sale* to Kyla and she seems to enjoy it as much as I once did. I wonder if thirty years from now she will see *Caps for Sale* on a library shelf and have the same reaction I had. And maybe when she enters the room of her children, she will say to them what I now plan to say to her: "Tss! Tss! Tss!"

To learn to read is to light a fire; every syllable that is spelled out is a spark. —Victor Hugo

Day 80

Mandavoluntary

"**K**yla, you have done such a great job with the flashcards that we got you a new study program!" I say.

Motivation? Manipulation?

"This new program is called *Hooked on Phonics,*" I continue, showing her the copy I checked out from the library. After three months of daily flashcards, often multiple times per day, Kyla has completed *YBCR*—memorized 100 or so words. Phonics seems like the obvious next step.

"And guess what! See this progress chart! When you complete this program, guess where we're going?" Kyla's favorite movie is *Madagascar 3,* and her favorite part of the movie is the circus. She is obsessed with all things circus. I know what she will say next.

"We're going to get ice cream!" Kyla responds. She also loves ice cream.

"We're actually going to the circus, a real circus—with a trapeze and animals and dragons." The Ringling Brothers are putting on a "dragon" circus nearby and given that I have never been to a circus myself, we decided to plan a family outing around Kyla's new study program.

Bribery?

Kyla's response is immediate—she launches into a "circus" dance, which is a slight variation on her other dances: the "I just went potty" dance, the "I'm eating a cookie" dance and the "We're about to go swimming" dance.

I open the book and we start the program. Slowly. Just like *YBCR*.

Kyla can now memorize words quickly, but stringing words together is still a struggle, notwithstanding the phonics DVDs she's been watching. The new program also requires effort on Kyla's part. After sounding out the first few words, she gets bored and walks away from the table.

As she walks away, I think of Amy Chua, the Yale law professor, whose book *Battle Hymn of the Tiger Mother* set off a national parenting debate. Chua claims that nothing is fun for children until they're good at it, and the only way to get good at something is to practice. But children don't like to practice and thus parents must override the children's preferences, at least early on. Once children become good at an activity, the activity becomes fun and the children get praised for their accomplishments, making it even easier to practice. Thus, a virtuous cycle is created.

Kyla has gained confidence from *YBCR*—she beams with satisfaction every time she finishes a lesson. Once we got past that initial struggle with *YBCR*, the virtuous cycle emerged, just as Chua predicted.

"Don't push your children," goes the conventional wisdom, "or else they will rebel." But as I think back to my experience in school, work, and athletics, it seems the opposite is true. The more my parents, coaches, and teachers pushed me, the more I excelled—especially when I knew that they cared about me. The higher the standard I was held to, the more I achieved, and the more I realized that I could achieve. I gained confidence from achievement and want to instill that same confidence in Kyla—help her do something that she thinks she can't do. Or doesn't want to do, yet.

March 2004 - Five years before Kyla's birth

"Well the dream is dead," I told my friend Shaheen on the phone. My tryout for a Division I football team had just ended. I was much slower and weaker than I had realized. I actually felt relieved though. I had paid a heavy cost chasing my football dream: two season-ending knee injuries, one surgery, two different junior colleges, and the two-year hiatus to South America in between.

*Children want the same things we want: to laugh,
to be challenged, to be entertained and delighted.*
—Dr. Seuss

Day 87

Overriding Preferences

"Keshia, how do you feel about making study program a daily requirement for Kyla?" I say. Keshia and I are lying in bed together at the end of the day, about to fall asleep.

Keshia doesn't immediately respond. Moments later, she breaks the silence. "Force her to do it like we agreed not to?"

"More like override her preferences in the short run so that she can benefit in the long run," I reply. Keshia has also read *Battle Hymn of the Tiger Mother* and knows what I am referring to.

"Nate, from the beginning I've been uncomfortable with the idea of forcing a program on her."

"I was, too. I never wanted to force her do the program either. But as I've seen her progress these last few months and watched how much she has enjoyed the program, I can't help but think that she'll continue to gain even more confidence if we keep up with the program."

"But why not just keep up with the program in the same way? Why do you need to start forcing her to participate? You said it yourself, she's progressed a lot these last few months and we've never forced her to do anything." The true ingenuity of the *YBCR* program is that Kyla is able to learn the words without me quizzing her. All she has to do is watch me—participate passively.

"Because I think Kyla is in a different place now than when we started. When we first started *Your Baby Can Read*, Kyla was unable to read anything—it would have been pointless to make her try. But she's learned her letter sounds now and is capable of sounding out words. I think we can ask more of her because she's capable of more."

"But the idea of forcing her to read just doesn't sit well with me," Keshia says. "I don't want to be the over-ambitious parents."

"I felt the same way until I started thinking about all of the other things we make her do. We make her take a nap every day. She has to eat her vegetables. She has to brush her teeth. She has to go to the bathroom every night before bed. We make her go to bed at bedtime. She'd rather not do any of those things, but we believe all of those things are good for her, so we make her do them."

"Yeah, but those are different, they're basic necessities."

"And reading is one of the most valuable skills she will ever possess. It's illogical to force children to do something they are incapable of. But now that Kyla can sound out words, why not hold her to a standard that she is capable of?"

"Because she's two. For fear that all of this backfires and makes her hate reading," Keshia responds.

"I admit that there are risks in forcing her to read—burnout being one. But in order for her to get good at anything, she's going to need to learn discipline and sacrifice. Dance practice wasn't always fun for you, but the performances were. And you've even said yourself that you wished your Mom had made you practice the piano more. Few things are fun until we're good at them."

"Yeah, but that was different. I was older then."

"Maybe that difference is crucial. But my point is that as parents we can feel good about holding Kyla to standards that she can meet. She is capable of sounding out words—we've seen her do it. But to be clear, I'm not talking about forcing her to read for an hour a day. I'm talking about five minutes per day. Five minutes in the morning when she has to practice sounding out words. We've seen in the last three months how much of a difference 5-10 minutes per day can make."

"And how do you plan on forcing her to read?" Keshia responds.

"The same way we get her to brush her teeth and go potty before bed—timeout. If she doesn't do what's required then she takes a little break from playing until she's ready."

"Time out for not reading?" Keshia responds.

"Not a send-her-to-her-room timeout. More of a let's-take-a-break-together-until-you're-ready. As her parents, it's our responsibility to help her be successful. And without discipline, there is no success. I think this program is a great way for us to begin instilling the principle that disciplined practice is the key to success in anything in life. And I agree whole-heartedly with Amy Chua that children gain self-confidence not from being coddled but from achieving. I gained confidence from my success in athletics, and you gained confidence from your success in dance. I think that making study program a requirement is a great way for Kyla to develop both self-confidence and discipline."

"Chua might be right about how children gain self-confidence," says Keshia, "but I'm not convinced the reward is worth the cost. I know what you're going to say though…that we should just 'try it' and see how Kyla responds."

"I won't do it unless you're on board. But I don't think it will be that big of a deal. Plus, reading is more fun than brushing teeth."

"Let's hope it stays that way. Let me think about it for a few days."

"We can always stop if we don't like where it heads."

A book is the only place in which you can examine a fragile thought without breaking it, or explore an explosive idea without fear it will go off in your face. It is one of the few havens remaining where a man's mind can get both provocation and privacy.
—Edward P. Morgan

Day 94

Turning Point

"**W**hen I get bigger I will get pregnant, have boobs, and sit in my own seat," Kyla says with a sigh as she climbs into her high chair for breakfast. Keshia is eight months pregnant and Kyla is intrigued by all things pregnancy. Kyla is also tired of sitting in her high chair.

"You're absolutely right," I quickly respond while suppressing a laugh. "And you could even do those three things in a different order if you want to."

"Yeah, but I'm not an adult yet, I'm just learning," she says, repeating one of her stock lines.

"We're still learning too, Kyla. Even as parents," I say. "But guess what! Guess what you get to learn today? We get to do the new study program, the one from the library: *Hooked on Phonics*."

"Nah" she casually responds, shaking her head. "I don't want to do study program today."

"But Kyla, it's fun, and I want you to be able to go to the circus.

"No." she repeats, turning to look me in the eyes.

"But this an educational program, remember? This is teaching you how to read. You want to learn how to read, don't you?"

"Noooooo!" she says while shaking her head.

"Remember how you get to go to the circus when you finish this program?"

"No! No! No!" her head bobbing with each exclamation.

"Kyla" I say calmly. "You need to do your study program for just a couple minutes, because it is teaching you how to read, and reading is one of the most important things you will ever learn. Study program is something we do every day—it's just like brushing our teeth, or naptime, or bedtime. If you're not ready to do study program right now, we can take a quick break together until you are ready."

"Nooooo!!! I don't want to go to timeout," she whimpers, as the tears begin to form in her eyes. Keshia flashes me a questioning look, and I can see the regret in her eyes for signing off on this. I don't feel regret in the moment, only after the fact.

"It's okay, Kyla," I say softly as I put my hand on her head reassuringly. "I can see that you don't want to do study program, and you especially don't want to go to timeout. But we do study program every day for just a few minutes, and if we're not ready to do it right now, we can take a quick break together until we are ready." In my mind's eye I see Tiger Mom Amy Chua looking on with approval— and my own mother turning away in disgust.

"I don't want to do study program!" Kyla shouts, kicking her legs.

"Okay, that's fine, let's just take a quick break from breakfast," and I pull her chair away from the table and stand by her. She starts crying, all the while I keep telling her that I love her, and that I understand why she is sad. She says she wants to get out of her chair, but I tell her that she needs to stay strapped in until breakfast is over. She cries harder, and I again repeat that I understand why she is sad, I am sorry that she is sad, but she needs to study for just a few minutes. "We study every day, and studying is one of the most important things we do. And after we're done studying, I can read you a few books if you want."

After a few more seconds of crying, Kyla suddenly composes herself and agrees to come back to the table. In fact, I am surprised at just how quickly she stops crying.

We complete the study lesson in just a few minutes, laughing and joking as if nothing has happened.

Our daily routine is set. Five minutes of study program every day.

March 2004 - Five years before Kyla's birth

My name was on the list! I had made the team! Coach Tidwell must have chosen me based on my junior college days, in spite of my tryout. I immediately walked to his office as directed.

"A 4.9 40!" Coach Tidwell said, as I took a seat in his office. "And you benched 225 pounds only one time?" he said in exasperation. "I took some heat for picking you, so please don't prove me wrong."

"I won't let you down, Coach. Thanks for trusting me. I won't let you down. I won't."

"Okay listen, because you are already a junior you probably won't ever play here. But you can at least be a practice team player for a year, and then we can reevaluate."

Babies are born with the instinct to speak, the way spiders are born with the instinct to spin webs. You don't need to train babies to speak; they just do. But reading is different. —Steven Pinker

Day 98

Canines and Kyla

My classmate, Vivek knows I enjoy social science, and he has sent me the promised email about willpower. I click on the link and start reading:

> Prisoners up for parole can be seven times more likely to get parole if they see the judge in the morning instead of the afternoon. The simple reason is "decision fatigue." Willpower is a limited resource, and when it is drained, people—and even

dogs—have less willpower for the next task in their lives.[11]

Seems logical, though I've never thought of it that way. I keep reading:

As a judge, it takes significant willpower to deliberately weigh all of the facts surrounding a prisoner's potential parole. When Israeli Parole Board judges got tired and hungry they often defaulted into denying parole, or in other words, doing nothing. Instead of agonizing over the decision to release a prisoner, the easier route was to avoid making a decision at all, especially one that would put a prisoner who might commit a crime back on the street. Denying parole preserves the status quo, leaving more options open—the judge can always grant parole in the future. Judges aren't alone though. Dogs, after obeying a "sit still" command for ten minutes, perform worse on self-control tests. Humans who resist the urge to eat a bowl of chips and salsa are more likely to give in to the temptation to eat ice cream later.[12]

My parents' advice to avoid temptation rather than resist it was wise beyond its years. And if we have a limited supply of willpower, it makes sense to do some of our most difficult tasks first thing in the morning. Like study program. During breakfast.

Until I feared I would lose it, I never loved to read.
One does not love breathing. —Harper Lee

Day 100

Digital Age

"**K**yla, I have a surprise for you tonight," I shout from the bedroom. "And it's on the iPhone." Surprises and the iPhone—I've just thrown another ball. Though we have completed the *YBCR* program, I still want to help Kyla memorize words, especially the sight words she is learning each morning during study program. I am sitting on my bed holding the iPhone when Kyla comes running in. She walks nowhere.

"Check out these flashcards on the iPhone!" I say. The free Sight Words app I downloaded is fully customizable. I open the app and the word "the" appears on the screen. "Tap the word Kyla and see what happens." Kyla taps the screen and hears my voice singing to the tune of Beethoven's 5th Symphony, "The! The! The! Theeeeee!"

Kyla giggles, taps the screen, and the recording plays again.

"Now check this out," I say as the recording ends. "Swipe your finger on the screen to get to a new word." Kyla swipes her finger and the word "with" appears. Without being prompted Kyla taps the screen, triggering the recording of my voice to the tune of the Itsy Bitsy Spider, "with with with with with with with with with with with with."

As we scroll through the twelve words I have inputted—all words from the morning study program—Kyla never removes her eyes from the screen. When we come to the end, Kyla looks up at me and says exactly what I expect, "Can we do it again?"

March 2005 - Four years before Kyla's birth

"We want you to switch from running back to receiver," Coach Reynolds informed me. I had trained anonymously for one year as a practice team player and hoped that with another six months of hard work I would be good enough to play in a game. Now I was supposed to switch positions? From my first football practice in seventh grade I had only played running back—partially because I couldn't catch, at least not consistently.

I'll learn to catch. Or never play.

I am a part of everything that I have read.
—Theodore Roosevelt

Day 102

Soft Spongy Sugar

"We're going to play a fun game tonight," I say to Kyla as I walk to the living room. The bag of mini marshmallows in my hand guarantees that I have Kyla's full attention. She runs into the living room, beating me to the couch.

"I'm making two piles of marshmallows. One pile will have only one marshmallow. The other pile will have ten. You can choose which pile you want to eat, but there's a catch. You can only have the larger pile if you wait fifteen minutes." I'm loosely replicating the famous Stanford Marshmallow Experiment, in which researchers found that four-year-old children who could delay gratification the longest ended up with better grades,[13] higher SAT scores, and even healthier BMIs.[14] They were also more popular and did fewer drugs.[15] Willpower, according to dozens of studies, is the single most important keystone habit for success.[16]

Kyla reaches for the pile of ten marshmallows but I stop her and explain the rules again. Then I give Kyla an idea, hoping to teach a lesson in self-control: "What if we distract ourselves while we wait for the fifteen minutes to pass? We could go for a walk outside or turn on some music and dance." At that, Kyla runs for the door. If self-control is such an important trait, maybe I can teach it, using both the marshmallow experiment and study program. In fact, research has shown that willpower developed in one part of life spills over to other parts of life. "A five-year-old who can follow the ball for ten minutes," said Todd Heatherton, a self-control researcher at Dartmouth, "becomes a sixth grader who can start his homework on time."

And maybe a three-year-old who can do study program for five minutes can become a four-year-old who can delay gratification for fifteen.

May 2005 - Four years before Kyla's birth

If I quit my summer job, practice football ten hours per day all summer and earn a scholarship, I will be better off financially than if I just work all summer—to say nothing of fulfilling a lifelong dream.

A children's story that can only be enjoyed by children is not a good children's story in the slightest. —C.S. Lewis

Day 112

Manatees and Fanatees

I chase Kyla to her bedroom for naptime. She never gets so chatty as she does before her nap—anything to postpone sleep—especially an iPhone filled with flashcards. Our three-pronged approach of phonics, memorization, and reading aloud remains relatively stable.

Kyla accepts the daily, five-minute phonics study program and Keshia and I accept that the study program requires patience and persistence. Kyla seems to enjoy it, though she also enjoys her Sundays off.

Memorization, now that we're using the iPhone, is bordering on addiction. And when Kyla is tired, absorbing sight words passively is much easier than learning information actively.

Reading books aloud together is the real pay out though.

"Kyla, we're going to read three *Elephant and Piggies* and then we'll do flashcards." She knows that naptime follows flashcards so she gladly complies—anything to delay the inevitable. The author of *Elephant and Piggie*, Mo Willems, is today what Dr. Seuss was fifty years ago. Gerald the elephant, Piggie, and Willems's Pigeon are only rivaled in popularity in our home by Kyla's imaginary friend Keleen. However, not even Willems holds a monopoly in our home. On a weekly basis, Kyla references Karma Wilson's *A Frog in the Bog*, Colin McNaughton's *Suddenly,* and Alice Schertle's *The Skeleton in the Closet.* The good books keep rolling in thanks to an occasional Google search for "best children's books."

I finish the three *Elephant and Piggie* books and Kyla requests *I'm a Manatee*, by John Lithgow. Kyla knows I'm a sucker for both Lithgow and her requests to read more books. Lithgow—the Harvard-educated, Lord Farquaad-voicing, Tony Award-, Golden Globe Award-, and Emmy Award-winning singer/actor—is now my favorite author. Lithgow's *Micawber, The Remarkable Farkle McBride,* and *Mahalia Mouse Goes to College,* connect with both Kyla and me but on different levels. Lithgow's other books, *The Runaway Pancake*, *Marsupial Sue*, *I Got Two Dogs*, and *I'm a Manatee,* all of which contain original scores that get stuck in our heads for days at a time, are now staples in our car rides.

I begin reading/singing:

I'm a manatee,
I'm a manatee,
I'm every bit as wrinkled as my granatee,
No difference between my face and fanatee.
A noble manatee, that's me…

I finish *I'm a Manatee* and we transition to flashcards. My recorded voice has given way to grandma's, grandpa's, cousins', aunts', uncles', LMFAO's, Coldplay's, Adele's, Katy Perry's and even Kyla's.

The moment we finish the flashcards, Kyla has another request: "Can we read *The Gruffalo*?"

It is what you read when you don't have to that determines what you will be when you can't help it.
—Oscar Wilde

Day 113

YBCR BK

"Um, Keshia, I've got a question for you." Keshia has just finished putting Kyla to bed and walks into the living room where I am sitting. I am on the couch with a computer on my lap reading the news.

"How would you feel," I continue, "if *Your Baby Can Read* just went bankrupt?"

"Really?" she says, as her eyes widen. "I guess it depends on why they went bankrupt," recognizing my question as a statement.

"False advertising," I say. "In part, it was that 'small window of opportunity' line." The instructional DVD referenced a "small window" of early learning. Since when was there a small window to learn anything?

"They went bankrupt for that?" Keshia responds.

"Well that and claiming that the program could teach 9-month-olds to read." I say. "They could no longer afford to fight all of the false-advertising lawsuits."

"Yeah, I guess it just depends on how you define 'read.' 'Memorize' is certainly more accurate."

"*Your Baby Can Memorize* would have sold a lot less units," I respond.

"*Your Baby Can Bark at Flashcards* even less," Keshia says, eliciting a laugh from me.

"So how do you feel about them going bankrupt?" I ask.

"How do *you* feel is the better question?" Keshia responds. "You were the one who did the program. I just supervised."

January 2006 - Three years before Kyla's birth

"Nate, it's Coach Mendenhall here." This was the phone call I'd been waiting for. My junior season had just ended and I had started every game at wide receiver, including the bowl game versus Cal Berkeley—my best game of the season. Mendenhall continued, "I'd like to offer you a full athletic scholarship for your senior season."

There is more treasure in books than in all the pirate's loot on Treasure Island. —Walt Disney

Day 125

Lit List

As I gather up the library books, a feeling of nostalgia comes over me. Our vacation to Idaho is coming to an end and the library books symbolize a week of stories and laughter that we are about to dump into a rusty book-return bin.

When we arrived in Idaho Falls seven days ago, our first family outing was to the library. *Cool Daddy Rat,* by Kristyn Crow, gave us the sound effects that became the preferred mode of communication for the week: "shooby dooby doo dat, zowie zowie zoo zat, huggy wuggy boo bat, click clickety rat tat, cool daddy rat." Kyla's stuffed-animal mouse is now named "peeky squeaky," which is always followed up by a "who dat?" if anyone calls the mouse by its new name. *Plant a Kiss,* by Amy Krouse Rosenthal, will now be our preferred baby-shower gift for friends. *Plant a Kiss* is also responsible for Kyla's new nickname: Little Miss.

Reading with grandma, grandpa, and cousins has nearly ruined us for reading by ourselves.

I suddenly have an idea. I pull the library receipt from the book return bag and put it into my pocket. Writing down the titles of our favorite books will at least prevent me from throwing away some of the memories.

We've been reading to Kyla about an hour per day for the last few months—15 minutes each at breakfast, lunch, and dinner, and then 15 minutes before bedtime. All the reading has led to a virtuous cycle—the more good books we read, the more Kyla wants to read. The key is finding good books. The day she gets tired of books is the day we head back to the library.

The best book list we've found is the Theodor Seuss Geisel Award winners and runners up. The award is named after Dr. Seuss and given to the most distinguished book for beginning readers. In other words, kids actually like the books on the Geisel list, such as *Vulture View*, a 2008 honor:

Vultures smell the air.
They sniff, search, seek, for foods that…

…REEK!
Those fragrant flowers?
No, no.
That spicy smoke?
No, no.
That stinky dead deer?
Yes, yes!

We're yet to read another book with pictures of carcasses. And after reading hundreds of books about anthropomorphic ducks, pigs, cows, and hens, *Vulture View* is a welcome reminder that not all animals are walking, talking, teeth-brushing herbivores.

Move Over Rover, a 2007 Geisel honor, was our first Karen Beaumont. We've since read seven others, all of which have become favorites, especially *I Ain't Gonna Paint No More*! with its LeRoy Neiman-esque illustrations.

Vulture View and every Karen Beaumont will make our new favorites list. And every John Lithgow, Mo Willems, Karma Wilson and Aaron Reynolds is on the list. And every Amy Krouse Rosenthal, Jez Alborough, and Mac Barnett. Every Carolyn Crimi, Doreen Cronin, and Colin McNaughton. Every Chris Van Dusen, Julia Donaldson, Ian Falconer, and Peter Brown.

If you don't like to read…

That which we persist in doing becomes easier, not that the task itself has become easier, but that our ability to perform it has improved. —Ralph Waldo Emerson

Day 180

Rats 'n Amaze

During study program, Kyla learns "dr" and "tr" words—drum, drag, trick, and trap. One month has passed since Kyla completed the kindergarten program. She is moving through the first grade program rapidly. Even two-year olds—especially two-year olds—who practice something for 180 consecutive days will see improvement. And just like other humans, Kyla enjoys learning new things. She regularly protests nap time, bed time, meal time, potty time, bath time, grocery-story time, clean-up time, brush-teeth time, get-in-the-car-seat time, get-out-of-the-car-seat time, put-on-your-clothes time, take-off-your-clothes time, etc. But she hasn't protested study program in months. And she still loves filling out the progress chart.

We finish the five-minute study program, and I ask Kyla if she wants me to read a few library books. She picks up several from the ground—*The Three Ninja Pigs, Mitchell's License, The Little Bitty Bakery*, and *Frog and Toad are Friends*.

As Kyla picks up the four books, I remind her that study program is over and that we don't have to read if she doesn't want to. Though I want to encourage reading, I fear overloading her. Kyla says she knows that study program is over and wants me to read her the books.

We make it through the first three and then Kyla is off coloring.

Study program, rather than getting harder for Kyla as she learns more complicated words, has become easier—she seems to enjoy it more now than ever. The virtuous cycle predicted by Chua has emerged. Study program has become a habit. And habits, according to *The Power of Habit*, require very little effort.

M.I.T. researchers placed rats at the bottom of a T-shaped maze and chocolate at the top left corner and then measured the rats' brain activity as the rats searched for the chocolate. At every sniff and scratch, the rats' brains exploded with activity.

As the researchers repeated the experiment again and again, the rats gradually quit making wrong turns and started finding the chocolate faster and faster, just as expected. However, when the researchers analyzed the brains of the rats again, they were surprised to see that brain activity had not increased as expected but had decreased. As the maze became easier, the rats started thinking less and less. Their behavior had turned into a habit.

The researchers concluded that our brains continuously strive to save energy. By developing habits, our brain is allowed to transition into autopilot, freeing us to focus our attention on other things. Compared to how easy it is to drive a car now, it's hard to believe how much mental energy it took when I first got my license.

Kyla now accepts study program without thinking—it's a habit.

October 2006 - Three years before Kyla's birth

My Law School Admission Test (LSAT) score confirmed what my ACT score told me in high school: my intelligence was just above average. So much for law school.

I cannot remember the books I've read any more than the meals I have eaten; even so, they have made me. —Ralph Waldo Emerson

Day 304

Are Nerds Always Unpopular?

"**D**o you think we're doing Kyla a favor?" Keshia asks as she climbs into bed next to me. It's a cool January night, and the brisk Bay Area breeze floats through our always-open window. Earlier that morning, Kyla finished the Hooked on Phonics First Grade program, earning a trip to "Dis-ley-nand." Or rather, we had been planning a family vacation to Disneyland for months when we realized that a vacation was a horrible thing to waste.

Can bribery teach children the connection between hard work and rewards?

"I have no doubt there are downsides to all of this," I respond.

"Yeah, like she'll be bored out of her mind during kindergarten," Keshia says. Kindergarten is still three years away—Kyla has just turned three, but her September birthday means she will start school just before turning six. Tomorrow she will start the second grade Hooked on Phonics program.

"She'll be bored at times, sure, though she won't be the only one."

"Yeah, but she'll be bored on a completely different level," Keshia says. "I'm thinking she should skip kindergarten, or at least start school a year early." Kyla, and the new addition to our family, baby Bennett, are asleep in the adjacent bedroom—window always closed to prevent them from hearing us.

"Maybe she should skip a grade, but there's more to kindergarten than learning to read. The social and emotional aspects are just as important as learning to read, and she'll be no more advanced socially and emotionally than anyone else. Not to mention physically…" I say, not finishing my sentence. I am 5'9" and Keshia has always been off-the-charts small.

"Yeah, but if we don't put her ahead, she might be an outcast for being a know-it-all."

"She might be," I say. "But as long as she's nice to other children, she can't be that big of an outcast can she? And lately she has been answering our what's-the-most-important-thing-in-the-world question correctly," I say half-jokingly. When we first asked Kyla the over-the-top question a few weeks ago, she responded, "Practice." Every day since then, she has given us the answer she knows we want to hear: "Being nice to other people."

"But being a know-it-all" I continue, "could also cut the other way. There's all that research that says if her teacher thinks she's smart, her teacher will support her more—provide her more feedback, call on her more, and challenge her more—which will boost Kyla's confidence and intelligence."[17]

"Unless becoming the teacher's pet furthers her outcast status?" Keshia responds. "Nerds are not popular, remember," Keshia says with a smile, referring to my favorite Paul Graham article, "Why Nerds are Unpopular."[18] Graham claims that in the adult world, hierarchy is determined by measurable output—those who are the best end up being the leaders. But in schools, where teachers and students often just go through the motions, output is hard to measure, much less agree upon. And when hierarchy is created without meaningful criteria, "we say that the situation *degenerates into a popularity contest.*"

"True. But remember," I say, "being popular takes time and effort and nerds would rather use that time to be smart. I would hope Kyla would make the same choice if she has to choose between the two. There are worse things than being a nerd."

"Yeah, like having no friends in kindergarten."

I don't respond—I share Keshia's concern. At the rate Kyla is going, she could be reading Harry Potter while some of her classmates are learning the alphabet. That might not spell friendships.

A moment later Keshia continues, "Do you feel like we're gaming the system?"

"I don't know," I say. "I'm ambivalent about all this. It's our responsibility to help her in every way we can—and the research shows that early reading success usually leads to later reading success. In that light, I sympathize with parents who 'redshirt' their children." Redshirting, holding children back a year in hopes that they would benefit from being the oldest, had become common after Malcolm Gladwell popularized the theory of *accumulative advantage* in *Outliers.*

"But from a societal, egalitarian perspective," I continue, "the children who are redshirted are the ones who generally need it the least. And statistically speaking, given Kyla's September birthday, she may be one of those who needs an advantage the least."

Neither of us say anything for a moment.

"But I don't feel like we're gaming the system," I continue, "because we're not doing all of this to get Kyla into Stanford. We don't even know if any of this will actually benefit her academically. I'm doing this—I think—because I want to teach Kyla that she can do hard things with hard work. My bigger fear is that she will think that knowledge falls out of trees, not realizing how hard she's worked to get where she is. I'm afraid she'll think she's smart, rather than think she's a hard worker," I say, referring to Carol Dweck's *Mindset* research.

"So we want Kyla's teachers to think she's smart so that they treat her better, but we want Kyla to think she's a hard worker, to encourage the growth mindset," Keshia says.

"Yeah," I say. "I had never thought of it like that, but, yeah, I think that's right."

"Do you ever think that you are overthinking this?"

"All the time."

Silence again.

"But then I think about those studies that found that parental involvement has a more powerful effect on academic performance than the school children attend, the effort of the teachers, and even the effort of the children themselves.[19]

"Yeah, but then I think about all those stories of crazy, over-ambitious parents who run their kids into the ground," Keshia responds.

No response.

Books are the quietest and most constant of friends;
they are the most accessible and wisest of
counselors, and the most patient of teachers.
—Charles William Eliot

Day 315

My First Invention

It's bedtime and Kyla is protesting. We've read books, done flashcards, and read more books. Now she wants to eat. And then drink. And watch TV.

I don't blame her—I hated going to bed every night as a child. I could never fall asleep quickly enough, and inevitably ended up in a state of panic each night, alone in the dark, angry that I would be tired in the morning. This routine repeated itself day after day, month after month. Finally, my parents made a simple suggestion: keep the same bedtime, but read with the light on until I fall asleep. This suggestion led to a string running from my bed, along the floor, to the light switch on the wall. Once I was on the verge of sleep, I wasn't about to risk raising my heart rate unnecessarily by standing up.

Allowing me to read at night might have been the best decision my parents ever made in raising me. Suddenly I was excited to go to bed; nighttime became a sanctuary for me. No matter what happened during the day, I could always rejoin my friends, Stuart Little, the BFG, and Frank and Joe Hardy.

"Kyla, what if I let you keep *A Million Chameleons* in your bed tonight?" Kyla smiles, falls to her mattress and pulls her blanket on top of her. I hand her the book and she hardly notices me leave.

Moments later, as I walk past her room, I hear her muffled voice and rustling pages.

December 2006 - Three years before Kyla's birth

"Nate Meikle Mountain West All-conference Team," read the press release. My senior season had come to an end, and I had done it—played Division I football as a scholarship athlete. But what if I had believed in myself sooner? My teammate John Beck, whose goal had been the NFL from childhood, would soon be drafted. What if I had set my goals higher, sooner?

A great book should leave you with many experiences, and slightly exhausted at the end. You live several lives while reading. —William Styron

Day 330

Aaaaaaaahhhhhhhh!

W e sit down for lunch and Kyla requests Marla Frazee's *Roller Coaster.* I can't remember the first time we read the book, but it did contribute to one of my most treasured memories.

I begin reading:

All of these people are waiting in line for the roller coaster. Most of them have ridden on lots of roller coasters. Some of them have only ridden on a roller coaster once or twice. At least one of them has never ridden on a roller coaster before. Ever.

Kyla points to the nervous little girl in red at the front of the line. The girl is clasping her dad's wrist with one hand, the other hand heading to her mouth for comfort. Other people are in line—an older couple, both hunched over at the waist; two cheerleaders, both laughing; and a weightlifter, calm and collected. But Kyla isn't interested in any of them. She is only interested in the first-timer in red at the front of the line.

We turn the page, and everyone is on board. The roller coaster heads down the first drop and the grandmother raises her hands, the cheerleaders scream in delight, the weightlifter puts his head in his hands; and the little girl in front, who was previously terrified, is now in a state of ecstasy, eyes closed, arms spread to the sky. Coming out of the final loop, the riders let out a collective scream—a scream I act out for the fifteenth time. As the ride ends, the little girl looks to her dad and says the words that always come at the end of a great ride: "AGAIN!"

I never thought much of this book until our recent trip to Disneyland. We met Rapunzel, rode Mickey's Fun Wheel, and ate at Flo's V8 Diner. We watched Aladdin, ate churros, and bought a Lightning McQueen souvenir. But there was only one moment during our entire trip when I saw Kyla in a state of uninhibited ecstasy: on the roller coaster.

If not for Frazee's book, I doubt Kyla would have even dared set foot on the ride. But not only did she get on, she screamed in delight from beginning to end. She knew what to expect—she had experienced a roller coaster in her mind a dozen times—had placed herself in the shoes of that little girl in red and overcome her own fears. It's no surprise that those who read fiction tend to be more empathetic than those who don't.[20] In the words of George R.R. Martin, "A reader lives a thousand lives before he dies. The man who never reads lives only one."

As the coaster raced down that first drop, I pulled out my camera just in time to capture Kyla's elation. And moments later when Kyla realized the ride was coming to an end, she finally let out her first intelligible word, "Noooooooooooooo!"

As we climbed out of the cart Kyla looked at me, her eyes shining, and said the word that I knew was coming: "AGAIN!"

*To see the video clip of Kyla on the roller coaster, scan the following QR code:

The great objection to new books is that they prevent our reading old ones. —Joseph Joubert

Day 371

HOP vs. BB

"Remember when we thought *Bob Books* were *the* answer to teaching Kyla to read," I say to Keshia. She's uploading a video of Kyla reading *Guess Again?*[21], an all-time favorite. Kyla, at age three and half, has just finished reading the 200-word book to Bennett. She's been practicing reading for a year now.

"I do remember *Bob Books*," Keshia responds, "because I saved us $150 by making you borrow them from the library." As good as the phonics-based *Bob Books* were, they had soon become just another one of the hundreds of books we read—a helpful, but small piece of the puzzle.

"Yeah, that was back when I was still in book-purchasing mindset," I say. We had soon realized that buying books wasn't the right approach. Variety was. From the library. We were going through 25 new books per week, reading the best of those 3-5 times each. Rather than buy books, we kept a list of our favorites, and rechecked them out months later, following the advice of C.S. Lewis: "It is a good rule after reading a new book, never to allow yourself another new one till you have read an old one in between."

Even the best books got boring for all of us eventually. But ten minutes per week on Google searching for "best toddler books" was sufficient to keep the good books rolling in. Asking librarians for recommendations was also crucial. And I just found my new favorite book list: The IRA's Children's Choices[22] — as voted on by 12,000 children.

As a rule, we never finish boring books—we don't finish drinking sour milk just because we start it. There are too many good books to waste time on boring ones, though boring books aren't to be mistaken for age-inappropriate books—*Where the Wild Things Are* at age two was a miss, but at age three was a homerun.

"*Bob Books* were good though," I say. "Especially when Kyla was younger." They had taught 100,000 children to read by 1993. And that was before the article in USA Today *really* made them popular.[23]

"And the corresponding app was even better," responds Keshia. The app was a phonics-based, interactive e-book that Kyla had played with for hours.[24]

"Looking back though," I say, "it seems so naive to think that just one reading program would have had all the answers. Aside from persistence, variety was the most important aspect of teaching Kyla to read."

"To a point," says Keshia. "Variety was important in the library books and DVDs. But you used Hooked on Phonics every day for nine months. There's not much variety there. Using *Bob Books* for 'study program' would have worked just as well I bet."

I pause for a moment before nodding. "Yeah. True."

May 2009 - Four months before Kyla's birth

If I apply the same effort to the LSAT that I applied to football, I wonder if I could qualify for a top law school. Several years had passed since I first took the LSAT and I was reconsidering law school. If I quit my job and study for ten hours per day for two months and I earn a scholarship to law school, I will be better off financially than if I work those two months, to say nothing of the advantages of attending a top school.

"How did you get the expertise to be the chief technology officer of a rocket ship company?" Scott Pelley, the 60 Minutes correspondent, asks billionaire entrepreneur Elon Musk.

"Well, I do have a physics background. That's helpful as a foundation. And then I read a lot of books and talked to a lot of, a lot of smart people."
Musk made his first fortune as an executive at PayPal. Most recently he founded SpaceX, the first private company to make a roundtrip flight to the space station.

"You're self-taught?" Pelley continues.

"Yeah. Well, I-- self-taught, yes, meaning I didn't, I don't have an aerospace degree."

"So, how did you go about acquiring the knowledge?" Pelley, incredulous, cannot accept Musk's first answer. But Musk persists.

"I read a lot of books, talked to a lot of people, and have a great team."[25]

Day 390

Teaching Reading IS Rocket Science

"How does Grinnell College," starts Thomas Friedman, "a small liberal arts school in central Iowa, where one in ten applicants are from China, choose perhaps 15 students from the more than 200 Chinese applicants?" I am at the Stanford Graduate School of Business listening to the *New York Times* columnist discuss his new book, *That Used to be Us*. Friedman continues, "Consider, for example, that half of Grinnell's applicants from China this year have perfect scores of 800 on the math portion of the SAT."

I have spent virtually no time thinking about Kyla and her SAT exam. I hope she will do well to give herself options, and I generally believe that what I do as her parent will affect how she does. As I listen to Friedman, my mind turns to a passage I recently read in Trelease's *Read-Aloud Handbook*: "The best SAT-preparation course in the world," said Tom Parker, the former admissions director at Williams College, "is to read to your children in bed when they're little. Eventually, if that's a wonderful experience for them, they'll start to read themselves." Parker claimed that he's never met a student with high verbal SAT scores who wasn't an avid reader.

What skill could be more valuable? Louisa Moats summed it up perfectly: "Teaching reading IS rocket science."

The man who does not read good books is no better than the man who can't. —Mark Twain

Day 411

The End of HOP

"**D**ouble five for finishing the whole study program," I say to Kyla as I raise my hands in the air. Kyla jumps and tries to hit my hands but misses both. She doesn't seem to notice though. She has just finished the second grade reading program at age three and is about to get her reward.

"Where are we going tonight, Kyla?" I ask.

"Ice cream!" she responds as she claps her hands and then kicks her right leg up behind her while raising both hands above her head.

I raise both of my hands again, and she connects this time.

"And what else are we going to get when we get ice cream?"

"A tooooy!" she says as she claps her hands and flips her leg again. When she completed the first grade program, her reward was "Disleynand"—tonight it's McDonalds. But she doesn't seem to notice the discrepancy.

Now that she has finished *Hooked on Phonics*, her new study program is to read one book during breakfast each day, six days a week. At this rate, she will enter kindergarten having read more than 700 books by herself, in addition to the 10,000 she will have listened to; she will also have resolved 10,000 conflicts vicariously.

"Kyla, do you love study program?" I ask her. I know what her answer will be, especially on a day like today.

She pauses. Looks at me. Doesn't say anything. And then runs to her toys.

My heart sinks.

April 2010 - Seven months after Kyla's birth

"Hi, is this Nate?" asked the voice on the other end of the phone call. "This is he," I answered as my heart started to race. It was my birthday but I didn't recognize the 650-area code. "This is Faye Deal, and I'm calling to let you know that we would love for you to join us at Stanford Law School this fall." The hard work had paid off—but I already knew that. The new LSAT score I had received several months prior proved as much.

The best moments in reading are when you come across something—a thought, a feeling, a way of looking at things—which you had thought special and particular to you. And now, here it is, set down by someone else, a person you have never met…. And it is as if a hand has come out, and taken yours. —Alan Bennett

Day 440

The Essay I Almost Wrote

"**I** found an essay this morning that I've been excited to show you all day," I say to Keshia as she sits down on the couch next to me. Sacred time has just started, and we are sitting in the living room. As I open my laptop, I continue, "One of the co-founders of Wikipedia wrote this essay. His name is Larry Sanger, and he earned his Ph.D. in philosophy from Ohio State. The title of his essay

is, 'How and Why I Taught My Toddler to Read.'"
I scroll to the Table of Contents and begin reading:

*Chapter 2: An eclectic method of teaching a
small child to read
Chapter 3: Phonics flash card method
Chapter 4: Your Baby Can Read
Chapter 5: Reading books*

Keshia smiles. "Where have I heard this method before?"

"I know," I respond, "including mealtimes even. That's when Sanger did most of the educational activities. But he never made study program mandatory, and his son was reading at a fourth grade level by age three years, four months."[26]

"Wow. So how did he do it without making it mandatory, and other than genetics of course?"

"Sanger just made it fun," I respond, ignoring the genetics comment momentarily. "And his son—like kids and humans generally—enjoy learning new things."

"Too bad you didn't come across Sanger's essay a year and half ago," Keshia says.

"Yeah, I had that same thought, but then realized how intriguing it is that we both did virtually the same things and got the same results. His essay summarizes a year-and-a-half's worth of my feelings and experience, yet we both arrived at the same place independently."

Sanger's 140-page essay is broken into two parts: 1) how and 2) why he taught his toddler to read, including a defense of his methods. I finish reading the table of contents to Keshia and say, "And here's Sanger's response to the criticism that his toddler can read thanks to smart genes:

> This conclusion does not quite fit the evidence. My wife and I do not claim to be geniuses (we have scored well on standardized tests, but not at super-genius levels). In terms of the learning potential of our grey matter, we think of ourselves as ordinary well-educated people. I have little doubt that my friends and family would be able to achieve similar results with their children…(T)he real debate is about whether we *should* teach our kids to read so early—not whether we *can*."

I then scroll to the over-ambitious-parent criticism and continue reading: "One of the most common skeptical reactions…to the very early teaching of reading is to dismiss it as the pathetic desire of ambitious, competitive parents for their children to 'win' and be the best."

Sanger believes that this response is rooted in the "lack of acquaintance with the people who actually use these programs," because in

Sanger's experience, the parents who used the reading programs were mutually supportive and unusually kind. The only thing that seemed different about them was "the strength of their conviction that they really can positively benefit their children by teaching them to read, and in other ways, from an early age."

The section on defensive parents— something that Keshia and I had both felt from some parents as we had shared our experience—was next. Sanger suspected that parents "resist taking early reading programs seriously because, if they did and their children were past toddlerhood, they might be inclined to conclude that they made a serious mistake as parents. After all (so you might think to yourself), if it is possible to give your children a four-year head start on reading, haven't you failed if you did not give them this opportunity? That's not what I think, but perhaps others have this worry."

This description matches our experience. The people who seemed most open-minded about our methods were expectant parents and parents whose children were under two. Sanger continued:

> This worry must be especially bothersome for early childhood educators and reading and child development experts: if there were

anything to programs like this, they in particular surely feel that they should have been on board. That is why, for professionals in the field, the cost of keeping an open mind about these programs, both emotional and intellectual, must be very high. It is no doubt much easier to dismiss such programs out of hand, ignore arguments and evidence, and endorse the usual views about reading readiness and the importance of play.

I then scroll to the final two paragraphs of Sanger's essay where he summarizes his motivation. I continue, "Sanger wasn't trying to create a 'genius,' and just teaching a toddler to read at an early age through flashcards would never create one." Sanger's real motivation mirrors my own:

There is almost nothing better in life than improving the mind with knowledge. Some of my happiest and most rewarding times in high school and college were when I was really learning. Deep knowledge is life-changing and character-changing. So "starting early" really has little more purpose to me than to improve the chances—not to guarantee, because there are no guarantees in life—that my child will do more of that sort of learning, and enjoy it, in the long run. That's why I have taught him to read early.

You think your pain and your heartbreak are unprecedented in the history of the world, but then you read. It was books that taught me that the things that tormented me most were the very things that connected me with all the people who were alive, or who had ever been alive. —James Baldwin

Day 450

Penguin Dancer

I'm asleep in bed when I feel a tap on my shoulder. I open my eyes and see Kyla standing next to the bed, wearing her full-body-suit penguin pajamas with her yellow tutu over top of her pajamas. She is also wearing her tiara from her recent ballet recital. It is Sunday morning, 6:30 am.

"I have a great idea," Kyla begins, as soon as she realizes I'm awake. "Maybe we could start doing study program on Sundays too," she says while beaming.

"That is a great idea," I respond. "Tell you what…if you want to read a few books today by yourself, you can. And let's definitely read a few books at breakfast."

"Deal," she says. She then turns and runs out of our bedroom into the bathroom, her castle.

July 2011 - Two years after Kyla's birth

I clicked submit to see my score. I had just finished the GMAT exam, but unlike the first time I took the LSAT, I now believed I was capable of scoring well through hard work. The score appeared on the screen and I pumped my fist. I had just qualified for every Ph.D. program in the country.

The reading of all good books is like conversation with the finest men of the past centuries.
—Descartes

Day 455

One Story Ends

I thumb through the Trelease book and stop on my favorite picture: Trelease sitting at the kitchen table, feet up, reading a book to his teenage boy who is doing the dishes. Trelease never limited his readings to fiction; if a magazine, newspaper, anthology, poem, or biography was interesting, that material became the day's read aloud. Regarding the weird looks Trelease got when people saw the picture of him reading to his teenage son, Trelease responded: "Now, if you have a preteen or teen who *doesn't* do the dishes in your home, then the child's IQ is higher than yours."

Children can listen on a higher level than they can read, so it makes sense to continue reading to our children through their schooling years. But why stop there? Reading *Where's My T-R-U-C-K* gets Kyla talking more than "How was preschool?" ever has.

Today is *Epossumondus* and *Corduroy,* Julia Donaldson and David LaRochelle, *Bubble Trouble* and *Children Make Terrible Pets*. Tomorrow will be *Les Miserables* and *Huckleberry Finn*, Nassim Taleb and Daniel Kahneman, *The New York Times* and *Sports Illustrated.*

Tomorrow will also be Dr. Seuss and Mo Willems. Bennett just turned one.

Kyla,

On February 5, 2009, when the nurse informed me that I would soon be a father, tears filled my eyes. Ninety-seven days later when I learned I was having a daughter, those same tears returned. I often look at the pictures from the ultrasound when we first saw your tiny hands and feet. I can see myself sitting by your mother's side waiting anxiously for you to join us as if our lives would only begin once you arrived.

And then, on that September morning when you finally took your first breath, tears of happiness filled my eyes yet again. In that moment, my happiness became inseparable from yours. From your first smile and first laugh, to your first word and first step, I have been by your side.

As a teenager, I always resented those parents whose lives seemed to be swallowed up in the lives of their children. "I will have enough cool things going on in my own life," I vowed, "that I will not need to live vicariously through anyone, especially my children."

How wrong I was. Not because I don't have enough "cool things" going on in my life—I have more interests now than ever. What I failed to understand as a teenager is that the joys of parenthood trump all other interests for me. I don't "need" to live life through you; I simply do live through you, at least in part. I feel your pain and happiness as I feel my own.

As you have come to realize while reading this book, I am ambivalent about putting you through study program at age two. In fact, we recently replaced mandatory study program with strongly-encouraged-but-voluntary study program. Ultimately we will never know how things would have turned out had we not taught you to read at age two. But, whenever you think about how much we emphasized education, I hope you remember what it symbolized to us: it was a way to connect and engage with you each morning, a way to share our love of learning. Above all, it was an expression of our love.

It has been said that little minds discuss people, average minds discuss events, and great minds discuss ideas. In my experience, the best way to fill our minds with ideas is to read a book—thus my emphasis on teaching you to read.

In that vein, I want to share an idea with you that I recently learned from a book: *Moonwalking with Einstein*, by Joshua Foer. The idea is a simple one: *We can lengthen our lives by creating more memories.*

In Joseph Heller's *Catch-22*, the pilot Dunbar concludes that if time flies when we're having fun, the surest way to slow time down is to make life as boring as possible. As reasonable (or unreasonable) as Dunbar sounds, he actually couldn't have been further from the truth, as demonstrated by the French scientist, Michael Siffre.

Siffre spent two months in total isolation in a subterranean glacier, with no clocks or daylight to mark the time. Without chronological landmarks or anyone to talk to, Siffre's days quickly melded into one another.

Yet when Siffre emerged from the cave two months later, he thought only one month had passed. Rather than time slowing down for him, time had sped up, by a factor of two.

"Monotony collapses time," concludes Foer. "Novelty unfolds it."

Siffre wasn't the first person to recognize this phenomenon however. William James, in the 17th century, observed that for children, every experience is new. But as children grow older, they convert more and more experiences into automatic routines until, "the days and the weeks smooth themselves out in recollection to contentless units, and the years grow hollow and collapse."

I don't want our years to grow hollow. I don't want our years to collapse.

Kyla, in an effort to lengthen our lives, and fill our minds with ideas rather than things, your mother and I have read thousands of books to you this last year. These books have become memories for us, and hopefully for you too. "If to remember is to be human," said Grand-Master-of-Memory Ed Cooke, "then remembering more means being more human."

When we started this journey, our goal was to teach you to read. But along the way, we realized that the time we spent reading together was what we valued most. Some of the books we read made us laugh (Mo Willems always delivered), others made us think (John Lithgow to thank), some even made us cry (*Sylvester and the Magic Pebble* got me every time). But every book we read together drew us closer. To keep these memories alive, I'm attaching the list of our favorite 250 books. These books are the ones that never got old, the ones we checked out over and over again—the ones that lengthened our lives.

Each time I review the list I relive the moments when we first read these books together. I hear your laugh, I see your smile, and I can't help but remember that the greatest gift I have been given was the chance to be a husband and father. And maybe someday these books will lengthen the lives of your own family.

"The great use of life," it has been said, "is to use it for something that outlasts it. That is the surest token of immortality." Your mother and I are using our lives—dedicating our lives—to you and your happiness. Through you, we live even after we die. And when that day comes, we hope you remember one thing about us: We loved you.

OUR FAVORITE 250 BOOKS

Fix-It Duck by Jez Alborough
Hit the Ball Duck by Jez Alborough
It's the Bear by Jez Alborough
Where's My Teddy? by Jez Alborough
The Acrobat by Gabriel Alborozo
Dancing in My Bones by Sylvia Andrews
Dirty Gert by Tedd Arnold
Hi! Fly Guy by Tedd Arnold
Parts by Tedd Arnold
No Dogs Allowed! by Linda Ashman
LMNO Peas by Keith Baker
Chicks Run Wild by Sudipta Bardhan-Quallen
Guess Again! by Mac Barnett
Oh No! Or How My Science Project Destroyed the World by Mac Barnett
Chloe and the Lion by Mac Barnett
The Adventures of Taxi Dog by Debra Barracca
Shark vs. Train by Chris Barton
Doctor Ted by Andrea Beaty
Doggone Dogs! by Karen Beaumont
I Ain't Gonna Paint No More! by Karen Beaumont
Move Over Rover by Karen Beaumont
Shoe-la-la! by Karen Beaumont
Where's my T-R-U-C-K by Karen Beaumont

Who Ate All the Cookie Dough? by Karen Beaumont
Journey by Aaron Becker
Rabbit and Robot: The Sleepover by Cece Bell
Madeline in America by Ludwig Bemelmans
Snip Snap!: What's That? by Mara Bergman
Bailey at the Museum by Harry Bliss
How Do You Wokka-Wokka? by Elizabeth Bluemle
Goodnight Moon by Margaret Wise Brown
Children Make Terrible Pets by Peter Brown
Mr. Tiger Goes Wild by Peter Brown
The Curious Garden by Peter Brown
Kel Gilligan's Daredevil Stunt Show by Michael
    Buckley
Cat's Colors by Jane Cabrera
Little Pig Joins the Band by David Costello
Henry & the Buccaneer Bunnies by Carolyn Crimi
Henry & the Crazed Chicken Pirates by Carolyn Crimi
Pugs in a Bug by Carolyn Crimi
Rock'n'Roll Mole by Carolyn Crimi
Click, Clack, Moo by Doreen Cronin
Diary of a Spider by Doreen Cronin
Rescue Bunnies by Doreen Cronin
Cool Daddy Rat by Kristyn Crow
Zombelina by Kristyn Crow
Carl's Sleepy Afternoon by Alexandra Day
The Day the Crayons Quit by Drew Daywalt
Jamberry by Bruce Degen
Llama Llama Red Pajama by Anna Dewdney
Bink and Gollie by Kate DiCamillo
Zombie in Love by Kelly DiPucchio

Driving My Tractor (Book & CD) by Jan Dobbins
Room on the Broom by Julia Donaldson
Stick Man by Julia Donaldson
The Gruffalo by Julia Donaldson
The Gruffalo's Child by Julia Donaldson
Where's My Mom? by Julia Donaldson
The Flea's Sneeze by Lynn Downey
Hank Finds an Egg by Rebecca Dudley
Mitchell's License by Hallie Durand
Cha Cha Chimps by Julia Durango
Burger Boy by Alan Durant
The Sleepless Little Vampire by Richard Egielski
RRRalph by Lois Ehlert
The Princess and the Pig by Jonathan Emmett
Olivia by Ian Falconer
Olivia and the Fairy Princesses by Ian Falconer
Olivia...and the Missing Toy by Ian Falconer
A Dragon Moves In by Lisa Falkenstern
Bark, George by Jules Feiffer
Tippy-Tippy-Tippy, Hide! by Candace Fleming
When No-one's Looking at the Zoo by Zana Fraillon
Roller Coaster by Marla Frazee
Corduroy by Don Freeman
Mice by Rose Fyleman
Dinotrux by Chris Gall
Dog in Boots by Greg Gormley
The Silver Button by Bob Graham
Chicken Big by Keith Graves
Blue Chameleon by Emily Gravett
Is Your Mama a Llama? by Deborah Guarino

Mimi and Lulu by Charise Mericle Harper
Chickens to the Rescue by John Himmelman
Duck to the Rescue by John Himmelman
Pigs to the Rescue by John Himmelman
Do Like a Duck Does? by Judy Hindley
Goldilocks and Just One Bear by Leigh Hodgkinson
Ten Red Apples by Pat Hutchins
The Little White Duck (Book & CD) by Burl Ives
Is it Time? by Marilyn Janovitz
Stuck by Oliver Jeffers
Rolie Polie Olie by William Joyce
The Hello, Goodbye Window by Norton Juster
I Want My Hat Back by Jon Klassen
I Need My Monster by Amanda Knoll
Bedtime for Mommy by Amy Krouse Rosenthal
Chopsticks by Amy Krouse Rosenthal
Little Oink by Amy Krouse Rosenthal
Little Pea by Amy Krouse Rosenthal
Plant a Kiss by Amy Krouse Rosenthal
Spoon by Amy Krouse Rosenthal
Yes Day! by Amy Krouse Rosenthal
Little Hoot by Amy Krouse Rosenthal
It's a Tiger! by David LaRochelle
The Best Pet of All by David LaRochelle
The End by David LaRochelle
Ten Apples Up On Top! by Theo LeSieg
Wacky Wednesday by Theo LeSieg
Ling & Ting: Not Exactly the Same! by Grace Lin
I Got Two Dogs (Book & CD) by John Lithgow
I'm a Manatee (Book & CD) by John Lithgow

Mahalia Mouse Goes to College by John Lithgow
Marsupial Sue (Book & CD) by John Lithgow
Marsupial Sue Presents The Runaway Pancake (Book & CD) by John Lithgow
Micawber by John Lithgow
The Remarkable Farkle McBride by John Lithgow
Pete the Cat and His Four Groovy Buttons by Eric Litwin
Pete the Cat: Rocking in My School Shoes by Eric Litwin
Frog and Toad are Friends by Arnold Lobel
Crunch Munch by Jonathan London
Marshall Armstrong Is New to Our School by David Mackintosh
Bubble Trouble by Margaret Mahy
Down the Back of the Chair by Margaret Mahy
Shhhhh! Everybody's Sleeping by Julie Markes
"Fire! Fire!" Said Mrs. McGuire by Bill Martin Jr.
Brown Bear, Brown Bear, What Do You See? by Bill Martin Jr.
Chicka Chicka Boom Boom by Bill Martin Jr.
The Monster's Monster by Patrick McDonnell
Even Monsters Need Haircuts by Matthew McElligott
I'm Bad! by Kate McMullan
Not Last Night But the Night Before by Colin McNaughton
Preston's Goal! by Colin McNaughton
Suddenly! by Colin McNaughton
We're Off to Look for Aliens by Colin McNaughton
When I Grow Up by Colin McNaughton

Martha Speaks by Susan Meddaugh
How Many Jelly Beans? by Andrea Menotti
Artichoke Boy by Scott Mickelson
Stay Awake, Sally by Mitra Modarressi
Nanny Goat's Boat by Jane Moncure
The Halloween Kid by Rhode Montijo
When a Dragon Moves In by Jodi Moore
A Friend for Minerva Louise by Janet Morgan Stoeke
The Little Bitty Bakery by Leslie Muir
Linus the Vegetarian T. Rex by Robert Neubecker
Chimps Don't Wear Glasses by Laura Numeroff
If You Give a Cat a Cupcake by Laura Numeroff
If You Give a Mouse a Cookie by Laura Numeroff
Fancy Nancy by Jane O'Connor
The King's Taster by Kenneth Oppel
Cooking with Henry and Elliebelly by Carolyn
    Parkhurst
Higher! Higher! by Leslie Patricelli
The Watermelon Seed by Greg Pizzoli
I Saw an Ant on the Railroad Track by Joshua Prince
Goodnight Gorilla by Peggy Rathmann
Officer Buckle & Gloria by Peggy Rathmann
The Day the Babies Crawled Away by Peggy Rathmann
How to Babysit a Grandma by Jean Reagan
How to Babysit a Grandpa by Jean Reagan
Moonday by Adam Rex
Carnivores by Aaron Reynolds
Creepy Carrots! by Aaron Reynolds
Here Comes Destructosaurus! by Aaron Reynolds
We're Going on a Bear Hunt by Michael Rosen

And to Name but Just a Few: Red, Yellow, Green, Blue by Laurie Rosenwald
Body Actions by Shelley Rotner
Bear and Bee by Sergio Ruzzier
Epossumondas Plays Possum by Coleen Salley
Vulture View by April Sayre
Skippyjon Jones by Judy Schachner
All You Need for a Snowman by Alice Schertle
Little Blue Truck by Alice Schertle
The Skeleton in the Closet by Alice Schertle
The Three Ninja Pigs by Corey Rosen Schwartz
The Stinky Cheese Man and Other Fairly Stupid Tales by Jon Scieszka
The True Story of the Three Little Pigs by Jon Scieszka
Cowboy & Octopus by Jon Scieszka
First the Egg by Laura Seeger
Abiyoyo (Book and CD) by Pete Seeger
Jerry Seinfeld Halloween by Jerry Seinfeld
Mr. Brown Can Moo by Dr. Seuss
Hop on Pop by Dr. Seuss
Ahoy, Pirate Pete by Nick Sharratt
It Looked Like Spilt Milk by Charles Shaw
Sheep Trick or Treat by Nancy Shaw
Sheep in a Jeep by Nancy Shaw
Hello Muddah, Hello Faddah by Allan Sherman
I'm the Biggest Thing in the Ocean by Kevin Sherry
Wombat Walkabout by Carol Shields
Suppose You Meet a Dinosaur by Judy Sierra
Turkey Trouble by Wendi Silvano
Robot Zombie Frankenstein! by Annette Simon

I'm Your Bus by Marilyn Singer
I'm a Duck by Teri Sloat
Caps for Sale by Esphyr Slobodkina
Little Mouse Gets Ready by Jeff Smith
A Sick Day for Amos McGee by Philip Stead
Sylvester and the Magic Pebble by William Steig
The Witches' Ball by D.J. Steinberg
The Little Red Pen by Janet Stevens
Brrr! by James Stevenson
We Can't Sleep by James Stevenson
Another Monster at the End of This Book by Jon Stone
The Monster at the End of This Book by Jon Stone
Silly Doggy by Adam Stower
Joseph Had a Little Overcoat (Book & CD) by Simms Taback
Here Comes the Big, Mean Dust Bunny! by Jan Thomas
Is Everyone Ready for Fun? by Jan Thomas
Rhyming Dust Bunnies by Jan Thomas
A Balloon for Isabel by Deborah Underwood
The Quiet Book by Deborah Underwood
Duck at the Door by Jackie Urbanovic
A Camping Spree with Mr. Magee by Chris Van Dusen
If I Built a Car by Chris Van Dusen
If I Built a House by Chris Van Dusen
Randy Riley's Really Big Hit by Chris Van Dusen
Happy by Mies Van Hout
The Museum by Susan Verde
Hide-and-Squeak by Heather Vogel Frederick

Captain Small Pig by Martin Waddell
Chester by Melanie Watt
Chester's Back by Melanie Watt
Chester's Masterpiece by Melanie Watt
Woof: A Love Story by Sarah Weeks
Boogie Knights by Lisa Wheeler
Castaway Cats by Lisa Wheeler
Art & Max by David Wiesner
The Three Pigs by David Wiesner
Falling for Rapunzel by Leah Wilcox
Waking Beauty by Leah Wilcox
Don't Let the Pigeon Drive the Bus! by Mo Willems *
Don't Let the Pigeon Stay Up Late! by Mo Willems *
Elephant and Piggie Series: Should I Share My Ice Cream? by Mo Willems *
Elephant and Piggie Series: There is a Bird on Your Head! by Mo Willems *
Goldilocks and the Three Dinosaurs by Mo Willems
Knuffle Bunny by Mo Willems
Knuffle Bunny Free by Mo Willems
That is Not A Good Idea! by Mo Willems
A Frog in the Bog by Karma Wilson
Bear Snores On by Karma Wilson
Hogwash by Karma Wilson
Moose Tracks by Karma Wilson
Sakes Alive! A Cattle Drive by Karma Wilson
The Little Mouse, the Red Ripe Strawberry, and the Big Hungry Bear by Audrey Wood
The Napping House by Audrey Wood
When I Grow Up by Weird Al Yankovic

A Few Blocks by Cybele Young
A Million Chameleons by James Young
The Hiccupotamus by Aaron Zenz

* All of the Mo Willems' *Elephant and Piggie* series and *Pigeon* series are favorites.

MEMORY MONTAGE

One year after writing the manuscript for *Little Miss: a father, his daughter & rocket science*, I made an eight-minute video montage summarizing the reading journey our family experienced together. The montage can be found at www.rocketsciencedaily.com or by scanning the following QR code:

FIVE STEPS WE USED TO TEACH KYLA TO READ

STEP 1: WE LEARNED THE RESEARCH

Decades of research show that the single most important thing parents can do to help their children become readers is to read to them.[27]
The last twenty-five years of reading research confirms that students who read the most, read the best, achieve the most, and stay in school the longest.[28]
The prime predictor of success for children entering kindergarten is a broad vocabulary.[29] Some children begin kindergarten having heard 48 million words. Others have heard only 13 million. However, a child who has heard 48 million words in the first years won't just have 3.7 times as many well-lubricated connections in its brain as a child who has heard only 13 million words. The effect on brain cells is exponential. Each brain cell can be connected to hundreds of other cells by as many as ten thousand synapses. That means children who have been exposed to extra talk have an almost incalculable cognitive advantage.[30]
Reading a book to a child exposes the child to three times as many rare words as a regular conversation does, and 50% more rare words than a television show.[31]
The brain is like a muscle. Individuals can improve their intelligence through practice.[32]
Children praised for effort and persistence tend to work harder and persist longer than those praised for intelligence.[33]

STEP 2: WE READ

We started reading to Kyla at birth as recommended by the American Association of Pediatrics.
We used the public library extensively. We did not have the money or space for the thousands of children's books we read.
So long as we had new, good books to read, we all enjoyed reading. The moment the books became boring, we checked out new (or old), good books.
"Good books" were those that all of us liked to read.
We reserved the best books from the library. By definition, the books checked in are the ones nobody wants.

We used book lists to find the best books:
     Little Miss 250 Favorites
     Theodor Seuss Geisel Award Winners and Runners Up
     International Reading Association Children's Choices[34]
     Jim Trelease Treasury

The more library cards in the home, the more library books the family can reserve.
We attended library read-alouds each week.
We asked librarians for recommendations.
We burned audio books to MP3 players and played favorite audio books in the car.
We turned on subtitles whenever Kyla watched movies.
We kept a list of favorite books. This helped us 1) identify favorite authors and 2) remember our favorite books, allowing us to check out favorites repeatedly.

STEP 3: WE TAUGHT MEMORIZATION

We started showing Kyla flashcards at age 2.5.
We showed Kyla flashcards, written in big letters, daily.

We used flashcard websites and tools:
  Your Baby Can Read
  ReadingBear.org
  BrillKids.com

We downloaded the free *Sight Words* app.
We customized the *Sight Words app* using our own voices, grandparents' voices, cousins' voices, popular singers' voices, Kyla's voice, etc.*
We checked out from the library *Meet the Sight Words* DVDs.
Above all, we tried to make flashcards fun.

*To see a video clip of how we customized the *Sight Words* app, scan the following QR code:

STEP 4: WE TAUGHT PHONICS

We started teaching Kyla phonics once she learned all of the sounds in the alphabet.

We checked out from the library or purchased the following:
  LeapFrog DVDs (e.g. *Letter Factory, Talking Words Factory, Talking Words Factory 2*)
  Bob Books
  Jane Moncure phonics books
  Hooked on Phonics programs

We spent 5-10 minutes per day practicing phonics.

Kyla was most excited, energetic and focused in the morning during breakfast.

We downloaded the *Bob Books* app and other phonics apps.

STEP 5: WE READ DURING MEAL TIMES AND BEFORE BEDTIME

Reading for 5-10 minutes at each of breakfast, lunch, dinner, and bedtime equals 20-40 minutes of reading per day.
Reading for 20-40 minutes per day equates to reading approximately 5-15 children's books per day.
Reading 5-15 children's books per day equates to 1,825-5,475 books per year.
Reading 1,825-5,475 books per year equates to 9,125-27,375 by the time children enter kindergarten.

ACKNOWLEDGEMENTS

I am grateful to all of the following who have shared ideas, commented on drafts, given me encouragement, and/or supported me in numerous other ways. Thank you all: Adam Grant, Amanda Secrist, Angela Pearson, Anthony Montague, Barbara Beck, Brianne Johnson, Brock Johnson, Bruce Rowe, Bryan Porter, Chad Lewis, Claine Snow, Cy Tidwell, Dane Godwin, Daniel Kuo, Daniela Saccone, Drew Manning, Elena Sudneko, Ginny Jenny, Heather Hutchinson, James Wigginton, Jen Lundeen, Josh Foster, Josh Waitzkin, Julie Geilman Mitchell, Judy Robinett, Julie Miskin, Justin Walker, Kathi Woodall, Kim Walker, Kris Anne Gustavson, Kylan Lundeen, Kyle Kahan, Linley Hutchinson, Lisa Burtenshaw, Liz Wiseman, Mark Rhodes, Michael Snapp, Mindy Leavitt, Nate Hutchinson, Nathan Garn, Necia Snow, Paul Gustavson, Phil Davis, Rachel Yu, Rebecca Davis, Rebecca Webb, Richard Hadley, Robin Thorn, Ryan Meikle, Ryan Thorn, Sahar Kahn, Stacy Kourlis Guillon, Stephen M.R. Covey, Suzanne Klahr, Talya Tabak, Terry Wade, Tim Hsia, Varsha Iyengar, Viola Canales, Vivek Viswanathan, Whitney Fogg, and Zach Rodgers. And above all, thank you Mom, Dad, Keshia, Kyla, and Bennett.

ABOUT THE AUTHOR

Nathan Meikle is a Ph.D. student in organizational behavior at the University of Utah where he researches groups and learning. Before starting his Ph.D. program, Nathan attended Stanford Law School, where he earned his Juris Doctorate. Nathan also attended Brigham Young University, where he earned his undergraduate degree in business. On fall weekends, Nathan works as an IMG Radio sideline reporter covering college football games across the country. Nathan lives with his wife, Keshia, and two children in Salt Lake City.

References

[1] Anderson, R. C. (1985). Becoming a Nation of Readers: The Report of the Commission on Reading.

[2] Trelease, J. (2006). *The Read-aloud Handbook.* Penguin.

[3] Hart, B., & Risley, T. R. (1995). *Meaningful differences in the every day experience of young American children.* Paul H Brookes Publishing.

[4] Zimmerman, F. J., Gilkerson, J., Richards, J. A., Christakis, D. A., Xu, D., Gray, S., & Yapanel, U. (2009). Teaching by listening: The importance of adult-child conversations to language development. *Pediatrics, 124(1),* 342-349.

[5] Christensen, C. M., Allworth, J., & Dillon, K. (2012). *How Will You Measure Your Life?.* Harper Business.

[6] Trelease, J. (2006). *The Read-aloud Handbook.* Penguin.

[7] Foer, J. (2011). *Moonwalking with Einstein: The art and science of remembering everything.* Penguin.

[8] Dweck, C. (2006). *Mindset: The new psychology of success.* Random House LLC.

[9] Dweck, C. (2006). *Mindset: The new psychology of success.* Random House LLC.

[10] Stanovich, K. E. (1986). Matthew effects in reading: Some consequences of individual

differences in the acquisition of literacy. *Reading research quarterly*, 360-407.

[11] Baumeister, R. F., & Tierney, J. (2011). *Willpower: Rediscovering the greatest human strength*. Penguin.

[12] Tierney, J. (2011). Do you suffer from decision fatigue?. *New York Times, August, 17*.

[13] Ayduk, O., Mendoza-Denton, R., Mischel, W., Downey, G., Peake, P. K., & Rodriguez, M. (2000). Regulating the interpersonal self: strategic self-regulation for coping with rejection sensitivity. *Journal of personality and social psychology, 79*(5), 776; Mischel, W., Shoda, Y., & Rodriguez, M. I. (1989). Delay of gratification in children. *Science, 244*(4907), 933-938.

[14] Schlam, T. R., Wilson, N. L., Shoda, Y., Mischel, W., & Ayduk, O. (2013). Preschoolers' delay of gratification predicts their body mass 30 years later. *The Journal of Pediatrics, 162*(1), 90-93.

[15] Duhigg, C. (2012). *The Power of Habit: why we do what we do in life and business*. Random House LLC.

[16] Tangney, J. P., Baumeister, R. F., & Boone, A. L. (2004). High self-control predicts good adjustment, less pathology, better grades, and interpersonal success. *Journal of Personality, 72*(2), 271-324.

[17] Jussim, L., & Harber, K. D. (2005). Teacher expectations and self-fulfilling prophecies:

Knowns and unknowns, resolved and unresolved controversies. *Personality and Social Psychology Review*, *9*(2), 131-155.

[18] Graham, P. (2003, February). Why Nerds are unpopular. Retrieved from http://www.paulgraham.com/nerds.html.

[19] Dufur, M. J., Parcel, T. L., & Troutman, K. P. (2013). Does capital at home matter more than capital at school? Social capital effects on academic achievement. *Research in Social Stratification and Mobility*, *31*, 1-21.De Fraja, G., Oliveira, T., & Zanchi, L. (2010). Must try harder: Evaluating the role of effort in educational attainment. *The Review of Economics and Statistics*, *92*(3), 577-597.

[20] Paul, A. M. (2012). Your brain on fiction. *Neuroscience*, *9*, 19.

[21] Meikle, N. (2013, April 25). Kyla at 3 Years 6 Months. Retrieved from http://www.youtube.com/watch?v=dtqZPa8lz4A

[22] International Reading Association. Choices Reading Lists. Retrieved from http://www.reading.org/Resources/Booklists.aspx

[23] Katy, K. (1993). Bob Books turns tots into readers. *USA Today,* June, *23*.

[24] Meikle, N. (2012, November 12). Bob Books App – June '12. Retrieved from http://www.youtube.com/watch?v=noVsqhSXYkw

[25] Pelley, S. (2012, March 18). Retrieved from http://www.cbsnews.com/news/spacex-entrepreneurs-race-to-space/

[26] Sanger, L. (2010, July 22). 3-year-old reading the Constitution - reading progress from age 2 to age 4. Retrieved from http://www.youtube.com/watch?v=cIu8BGFqMm4

[27] Anderson, R., Hiebert, E., Scott, J.,Wilkinson, I. (1985). *Becoming a Nation of Readers: The Report of the Commission on Reading.* Champaign-Urbana, IL: Center for the Study of Reading, p. 23.

[28] Stanovich, K. (1984). Matthew Effects in Reading: Some Consequences of Individual Differences in the Acquisition of Literacy. *Handbook of Reading Research.* Pearson, P. D., ed. Longman. (pp. 829-864). New York; Elley, W. B. & Mangubhai, F. (1983, Fall). The impact of reading on second language learning. *Reading Research Quarterly.* (pp. 53-67); Foertsch, M. *Reading In and Out of School.*

[29] Hart, B. & Risley, T. (1996). *Meaningful Differences in the Every Day Experience of Young American Children.* Baltimore, MD: Brookes Publishing.

[30] Christensen, C., Allworth, J., Dillon, K. (2012). *How Will You Measure Your Life?* Harper Business.

[31] Trelease, J. (2006). *The Read-aloud Handbook.* Penguin.

[32] Dweck, C. (2006). *Mindset: The new psychology of success.* Random House LLC.

[33] Dweck, C. (2006). *Mindset: The new psychology of success.* Random House LLC.

[34] International Reading Association. Choices Reading Lists. Retrieved from http://www.reading.org/Resources/Booklists.aspx

Made in the USA
San Bernardino, CA
05 December 2014